Praise for *Spir...*

"*Spiritual Maturity* is a book that ope... of life, including the highs and lows t... Unless we are willing to engage *all* ... ~~spirituality~~ is a contradiction in terms. This kind of openness leads us to resilience and joy, no matter what happens. A very wise book."

— LARRY DOSSEY, M.D., author of
Reinventing Medicine and *Healing Words*

Praise for *Living Our Dying*:

"Joseph Sharp's book . . . is like a Zen whack on the head, waking us to a vibrant and exuberant appreciation of life."

— THOMAS MOORE, author of
Care of the Soul

". . . a must-read for all conscious pilgrims and a superbly written gift."

— M. SCOTT PECK, M.D., author of
The Road Less Traveled

". . . a gentle 'how-to' which heals as it instructs."

— MARIANNE WILLIAMSON, author of
A Return to Love

"Joseph Sharp, from his rich perspective of AIDS survivor, minister, friend, lover, and spiritual seeker, offers heartfelt and honest encouragement to us to remain open and present to the profound mystery . . . of death and life."

— RAM DASS, author of
Be Here Now and *Still Here*

"It is truly unforgettable. An inspiring and rare contribution . . ."

— JOAN HALIFAX, author of
The Fruitful Darkness

". . . a profound book, but it is also witty, provocative, and practical."

— STANLEY KRIPPNER, Ph.D., professor of
psychology, Saybrook Institute

"Tender. Awesome. Wise."

— JEANNE ACHTERBERG, Ph.D., senior editor,
Alternative Therapies for Health and Medicine

SPIRITUAL MATURITY

*Stories and Reflections for the
Ongoing Journey of the Spirit*

Joseph Sharp

A Perigee Book

Perigee Books
Published by The Berkley Publishing Group
A division of Penguin Putnam Inc.
375 Hudson Street
New York, New York 10014

First edition: June 2001

Published simultaneously in Canada.

The Penguin Putnam Inc. World Wide Web site address is
http://www.penguinputnam.com

Library of Congress Cataloging-in-Publication Data
Sharp, Joseph, 1961–
Spiritual maturity : stories and reflections for the ongoing journey of the
spirit / Joseph Sharp.
p. cm.
Includes bibliographical references.
ISBN 0-399-52679-X
1. Spiritual life. I. Title.
BL624 .S485 2001
291.4'4—dc21   00-051043

Printed in the United States of America

10   9   8   7   6   5   4   3   2   1

For one of my heroes, my sister—
Lesley Hope Sharp

❧ CONTENTS

Acknowledgments   ix

(A Story in Lieu of an Epigraph)   xi

Introduction   xiii

25 QUALITIES OF SPIRITUAL MATURITY AND DEPTH

1. Sacred Individuality   1

2. Grand Permission   10

3. Daring to Be Spiritually Incorrect   17

4. Awe   27

5. Including It All   34

6. Cosmic Irony   48

7. Larger Faith   53

8. Soft Courage   58

9. Ongoing Evolution   68

10. Honoring Life's Complexity   78

11. Remembering You'll Forget   82

12. Outrageousness   87

13. Grounding Yourself in the Extraordinary   95

14. Talking Your Walk   102

15. Embracing Opposites and Contradictions   107

16. Discerning Love from Like   114

17. Personal Activism   118

18. Allowing Forgiveness to Take Its Time   129

19. It's Never Too Late   137

20. Inviting Fear to Tea   143

21. Letting Be, First   149

22. Innocent Misunderstandings   152

23. Practicing Without Preaching   162

24. Resting in Mystery   164

25. You Don't Have to Protect God from Yourself 169

   Afterword   177

   Notes   180

   About the Author   184

⊰ ACKNOWLEDGMENTS

I WISH TO THANK MY COMMUNITY OF FRIENDS, FAMILY, readers, and other kind souls who've supported me and my work during the process of this book. Here's my list:

First and foremost, there is one person who championed, guided, and encouraged this book (and me) more than any other and whose selfless grace continues to amaze me: M. Scott Peck, M.D. Scotty, may this book live up to your standards of honesty and truth, of embracing life's grit as well as grace.

Next, I must thank my literary agent, Jonathan Dolger, for his continued faith in this book and in my career as a writer.

I also need to thank those writers who endorsed my first book and many of whom I haven't yet been able to thank, formally, in print: Jeanne Achterberg, Angeles Arrien, Ram Dass, Larry Dossey, Joan Halifax, Stanley Krippner, Thomas Moore, M. Scott Peck, and Marianne Williamson. Your support and praise for my work is deeply appreciated. Also, thanks goes to Jean Richardson at Ghost Ranch Conference Center in Abiquiu, New Mexico, and the entire ranch staff for allowing me the space and freedom to put the ideas in this book to the test. And, of course, to all those who've attended my workshops at Ghost Ranch and elsewhere, my deepest gratitude.

And to these essential ones: My parents, Joe and Brenda Sharp—without you, I'd be lost. My aunt Martha Neill, a constant reminder of God's unknowable boundaries and the power of prayer—Mamie, I love you beyond words. My dear friend Marcia Tyson Kolb—Marcia, your counsel and late-night phone calls mean the world to me. Trevor Hawkins, M.D., and everyone at Southwest Care Clinic in Santa Fe—thanks for always being there when I need you. To these friends and/or loved ones who read parts or all of the manuscript over the last few years and gave me their opinions: John McDowell, Joan Logghe, Patricia Mullen, Martha Neill, and Sally Fisher—thank you all for your wisdom, advice, and care for this project. Also my gratitude to Mohan Jhass, Guinever Grier, Terry Arnn, Carl Michel, Bob and Donna Bost, Marc Perry, and David Rayon for their love and support in uncountable ways.

And, of course, to Jennifer Repo, my editor at Perigee, I cannot say enough. Jennifer, you have my deepest appreciation and gratitude for truly "getting" the book, for understanding it in some ways better than myself and helping me shape it into this final form. This book is very blessed to have such an editor and advocate—as am I.

"*I WANT TO SPEAK TO THE CHAPLAIN ALONE.*" *JIM LIFTED THE opaque oxygen mask away from his mouth as he whispered the words. Each breath was a gripping rattle as if trying to pull life itself out of thinning air. We all knew Jim wouldn't live through the weekend; his mother had arrived earlier in the day, friends were beginning to gather. This man in his mid-forties would be the second person to die on my unit within two weeks.*

Jim looked to his mom. "Alone," he repeated. Then he looked to me and winked.

I was an intern chaplain for the Infectious Disease Unit at Parkland Memorial Hospital in Dallas, Texas. A teaching hospital for the University's medical school, Parkland also serves as Dallas County's welfare hospital. Since the hospital had no official religious affiliation, its intern chaplaincy program was considered "interfaith"—meaning everything and nothing. Our patients ran the gamut from Fundamentalist Christian to Buddhist, from Voodoo to New Age, to no religion whatsoever. Such was, and is still, the diversity of Parkland.

"Well, Rev.," Jim said after the others had left the room. He called me "Rev." sometimes as a joke. He knew I wasn't ordained.

He knew that, as far as my internship at the hospital was concerned, I had no agenda nor affiliation with any particular religion. During the last few weeks, we'd discussed religious affiliation thoroughly. Jim had been a full-time choir director at a large suburban church before he became ill with AIDS.

Jim looked me directly in the eyes. Like a Zen master's slap or a cronish nun's wise focused stare, his deliberate glance cut through any pretense of what I called my "chaplain's costume"—those defenses I sometimes used to protect and distance myself. "I just want you to know something," he continued slowly, softly, gasping between each few words.

"I just want you to know if I could do it all over again, I'd be more outrageous. You know, give 'em more hell. Be more myself and less what everybody said I'm supposed to be. That's all. Just wanted you to know that."

Jim brushed a bony finger toward the oxygen mask and I helped him lift the plastic cup back, snug and fit to his face. I could see the smile from beneath the mask. His eyes twinkled now, vibrant, so alive within his dying body.

"More myself," he repeated softly. "More myself."

INTRODUCTION

How wonderful it would be to reach a place along our spiritual exploration where, once we've grown enough, God would finally throw up Her hands and say, "You've made it child, from here on out it's all icing on the cake; no more problems or troubles for you; no more lessons to learn; from now on it's just happiness, peace, love, and light all the way!" But the reality is otherwise. The journey of spiritual growth is an always ongoing pilgrimage of experience, from our first breath to our last and most likely beyond. There are always more lessons to learn, more depths to explore.

I believe this sense of continuous and progressive growth is what Jesus was hinting at when He told his followers that, in the future, they would have "greater works" of their own to accomplish. It is what the Hindu saint Ramakrishna was speaking of when he reminded his students, "No matter how high the bird flies, it can always fly higher. There is no limit to realization, because Truth is an infinite sky." Reversing the metaphor, we could just as easily say that no matter how deeply inward one dives beneath the surface of life's outer appearance, there is no limit to the soul's depths of discovery, as well. The Way is an ongoing journey of continued spiritual growth and maturation. Infinite sky, infinite depth.

If you're looking for the promise of finality—say, a list of quick, easy recipes to forever transform your life into a miraculous slice of sweet spiritual pie—you should know this is not the book for you. Don't get me wrong, the path is indeed filled with many wonderful, miraculous moments of joy. I'm no masochist—love, love, love, joy. But in my experience, life's real road is just as often filled with lessons that aren't so joyous. And some are downright awful, but nonetheless potent. As said above, I operate from the model that this learning process is pretty much ongoing all the time and we never reach finality, at least not while here on earth. For me, finality is not the point. Learning is. As is opening your heart and becoming a more truthful, compassionate, understanding, and loving person. As is being true to your innate calling, to what I like to call a person's "sacred individuality." So I think it's only fair that you know my model of the "ongoing journey" early in this book.

I also take a view of spirituality that is, well, inclusive. Though I'll always have a special place in my heart for the Christian tradition—like many of you, I was raised in it and resonate to its imagery and ritual in a way that is, for me, singularly powerful—still, I could no more limit my way of exploring life and spirituality to "Christian only" than I could proclaim I'd experience the world from a "male only" perspective. Like everyone I know, untold things create my perspective of life. Just to scratch the surface of the obvious: I'm a baby boomer and long-time survivor of HIV; I love reading literary novels but try not to miss any new episodes of *Star Trek*; I'm college-educated, awful when it comes to managing money, puckish yet fiercely loyal to friends, both a native Texan and a Leo, part Irish, Italian, English, and Choctaw; the list goes on. The reality is, I cannot help but simultaneously look at the world from many varied perspectives. And like most of you, I've come to believe we can safely learn from the wisdom offered by other traditions and cultures, by other religions and other faiths.

Over the last ten years, I've explored and refined the concepts and teachings presented in this book with a wide range of spiritually eclectic seekers—from brief evening lectures at local churches and libraries to the annual week-long workshops I host every summer at Ghost Ranch Conference Center in northern New Mexico. At these diverse gatherings, I've come to experience firsthand how a person's spiritual identity is not dishonored by the kind of inclusive, multi-faith approach this book explores. To the contrary, I've found that a seeker's belief, faith, and understanding are matured, empowered. Deepened. In other words, you become a deeper Christian, or deeper Buddhist, or deeper Jew, or deeper New Age spiritualist, or whatever. You become deeper, truer to the "spirit of the law" and way of your soul's authentic expression.

Here, however, it is necessary to make the distinction that *deeper* is not always *better*, especially in the eyes of the Established Way. Because it might be misleading to claim that by cultivating the spiritually inclusive view of honoring your sacred individuality, it will likewise make you a *better* Buddhist or Jew or Christian. It certainly might (and I believe it will). But these teachings could also be viewed—especially by those who resist any kind of questioning or imagination when applied to religious doctrine or creed—as too free thinking, too individualistic, perhaps even dissident. In the usual narrow sense of meaning, *better* is in the eye of the beholder. Whereas spiritual depth isn't about appearances. It is something you feel. Something you live.

One of my favorite stories speaking to this point comes from poet Rodger Kamenetz. During a trip to northern India to study Tibetan Buddhism, he found a spiritual connection was likewise deepening with his religion of origin, Judaism. After the experience, Kamenetz shared this ironical blessing with the Dalai Lama. Kamenetz said, "By making us look more deeply into Judaism, you have become our rabbi." The Dalai Lama responded with a chuckle and a smile, cupping his hand to the dome of his shaven head, saying, "So you will give me a small hat?" It's a brilliant image of inclusive and open-minded spiritual wisdom for us to contemplate: the great Tibetan Buddhist, His Holiness the Dalai Lama, sitting serenely upon his meditation cushion while sporting a silken black yarmulke. No, spiritual maturity and depth isn't about appearances—nor a xenophobic attitude toward one's own religious tradition.

Spiritual maturity is an always ongoing experience, and its teachings can arise any time, anywhere. And, thankfully, this growth can be encouraged, cared for, and cultivated. That's the intention of this book—to help encourage and cultivate your own individual experience of spiritual depth and maturity within your actual, everyday life. But how to do this? How do we explore this process without becoming arrogant or righteous? I've found that stories, for me, are the most helpful. Stories often speak at a depth of resonance that didactic commentary could never hope to reach. Because of the personally revealing nature of many of these stories, this book is also a kind of personal memoir. But only loosely. Unlike a true memoir, its goal is not to tell of my life, but to offer an imaginative point of view, a re-visioning of what is considered appropriate for the spiritual life. In experimenting with different ways of writing, I found the anecdotal nature of storytelling—personal myth—to serve this re-visioning best.

What follows are twenty-five stories and reflections that explore the qualities of this ongoing process of spiritual depth and maturation. These are qualities I believe to be somewhat universal, qualities I believe are present in the a maturing spirituality, regardless of religious affiliation or tradition. Each has taught me to pause, to reconsider, and to re-imagine my life's odyssey in a larger, more inclusive way. Each still reminds me of just how big God is, and so how big my experience as God's child could also be. Together they present a vision of the sacred that embraces life's enormity, contradiction, and mystery. They also call for us to muster the courage and permission to re-imagine some of spirituality's great themes—like faith, tolerance, forgiveness, and so on. Being true to one's sacred individuality means we must bring our own personal imagination, intelligence, and creativity into these great themes, so we might discover the infinite sky and bottomless well of what's within and among everyday human life experience for ourselves.

But why twenty-five?

Honestly, because twenty-five seemed like a good number. I could have shortened the list to a dozen or so, or extended it considerably. But I settled for a comfortable number where we might be able to cover those more basic qualities—like "Awe" and "Honoring Life's Complexity"—and still have the space to explore a few specialized lessons—such as "Discerning Love from Like" and "Allowing Forgiveness to Take Its Time." And though I obviously have chosen an order to present the qualities (and advise the first-time reader to read them in this order), it is important to understand that each chapter/quality is written so that it stands on its own as a complete and whole exploration. So also feel free to use this book in your own inspirational way, flipping open to a particular chapter that might speak to you at a given time.

Of course, when it comes to exploring spiritual maturation, no book could honestly claim to be definitive. There are always other, different—perhaps better—ways to express the same truth. So instead of promising definitiveness, this book aims to provide a kind of springboard for imagination and, above all, a continual sense of permission. That's another major theme of this book, *permission*. I've come to believe that permission and authentic spiritual depth go hand in hand.

Here's my hope, my prayer:

That the stories and suggestions in this book will help you deepen within your chosen spiritual tradition in whatever form that takes. That some of these stories will give you pause as they have me. And perhaps, on occasion, turn a few of your preconceived notions about the "spiritual" life upside down, allowing you more permission to freely express the sacred individuality that is authentic to your soul's unique path. More permission to discover the depth and maturity of your own spirituality and way through everyday life.

A wonderful, holy hope. Don't you think?

Joseph Sharp
Santa Fe, New Mexico

Direct your eye right inward, and you'll find

A thousand regions in your mind

Yet undiscovered. Travel them and be

Expert in home-cosmography.

THOREAU, *Walden*

25 QUALITIES OF
SPIRITUAL MATURITY AND DEPTH

1. Sacred Individuality

2. Grand Permission

3. Daring to Be Spiritually Incorrect

4. Awe

5. Including It All

6. Cosmic Irony

7. Larger Faith

8. Soft Courage

9. Ongoing Evolution

10. Honoring Life's Complexity

11. Remembering You'll Forget

12. Outrageousness

13. Grounding Yourself in the Extraordinary

14. Talking Your Walk

15. Embracing Opposites and Contradictions

16. Discerning Love from Like

17. Personal Activism

18. Allowing Forgiveness to Take Its Time

19. It's Never Too Late

20. Inviting Fear to Tea

21. Letting Be, First

22. Innocent Misunderstandings

23. Practicing Without Preaching

24. Resting in Mystery

25. You Don't Have to Protect God from Yourself

1

Sacred Individuality

Each life is marked by a uniqueness in personal character, experience, and expression, a one-of-a-kind soul.
This truth suggests a radical possibility: that the sacred, as expressed by humanity, can be as diverse and
multifaceted as we are as individuals.

WHEN I WAS IN THIRD GRADE, MY FAMILY MOVED TO
Cleveland, Texas, a town of about three thousand people,
some thirty miles east of Houston. Cleveland's main industry
was logging the Big Thicket of east Texas. The town didn't
have a square, but a strip of stores along the railroad tracks.
I'd never heard the word "redneck" uttered by my parents
until we moved to Cleveland.

Despite its cultural isolation (hardly any kid in my class-
room at school had ever made the whole half-hour trip to
Houston), Cleveland did have one great advantage. For the
first time in my life, we were able to watch the Public
Broadcasting Service on our family television set. This was
in the days before cable, so if you didn't live near a large
city, you didn't get PBS. When I found Houston's PBS
affiliate, I knew I'd finally come home. I didn't bother skim-

ming the surface with *Mister Rogers' Neighborhood* or *Sesame Street*. No, give me the depth of hard science and exploration. Turtles, dinosaurs, piranhas, snakes, the Loch Ness monster, outer space, the inner space of underwater sea exploration. I was like one of those sea sponges on *Jacques Cousteau*. I soaked it all up.

Once, over dinner with my grandparents, I proudly announced some new knowledge gleaned from PBS. I'd seen a medical documentary and, by comparing my preexisting symptoms, was able to make a self-diagnosis of my ailment. At age eight, I announced—just as my grandfather was passing the homemade drop biscuits around the dinner table— that I was experiencing the early stages of syphilis. My grandfather must have retold that story a hundred times before he died, his face turning tomato red from laughter. So I loved PBS, and we hadn't been in our new home for two months before I saw my first documentary about Charles Darwin and his theory of evolution.

Sitting on a couch pillow, positioned on the floor in front of the TV, it became so obvious to me. A slow, delicious smile blossomed inside my thoughts: "So *this* was how God did it!"

And, for the first time ever, it all made sense. I'd never wholly believed the "everything created in six days" story. What thinking kid would? The problem was glaring. Where did you fit the dinosaurs? We all knew they lived for millions of years and then became extinct. We all knew that was before man came onto the scene. So where did you fit that million years of dinosaurs into six days? Something had to give in the numbers.

But after watching PBS that night, it was so simply evident. God created man's soul in His "image" in those six days, but He created man's body over millions of years through a process Darwin called evolution. Simple. Besides, what's millions of years to God? Big intellectual sigh. I no longer had to secretly think the *Holy Bible* had been wrong all this time. I could hardly wait until the following Sunday so I could share my discovery in Sunday School.

When Sunday morning came, I was anxious. This was it. They would all be so grateful at my tremendous news. No one would have to pretend that it just didn't make sense anymore. Science had indeed stood up for God and helped Him smooth over a few holes in His story. So it was with this great anticipation and joy that I went to my third grade Sunday School class that warm spring morning.

Then . . .

(—no memory of what happened, of how I shared my insight, or of how my classmates and teacher responded to the splendid news; nothing; it's a blank; nothing but a sudden scene shift—from one moment, riding in the back seat of our family's metallic bronze Oldsmobile, with my sister and I both dressed in our Sunday best—)

. . . to me alone after Sunday School, my feet dangling

from a swing on the rusting swing set just outside the church. The swing set is made to hold five kids. I sit alone, the other wooden slat seats empty. Three boys, about my age, stand a few feet away. They chant, over and over, "Joe comes from a monkey, Joe comes from a monkey."

This was my first conscious encounter with the moralist literalism that is often present in our religious institutions. My Sunday School teacher and fellow students couldn't make the leap to consider that perhaps there was a spirit of the law that went beyond the letter. They couldn't allow for new ideas or inspiration to arise from a child's imaginative spirit. For them, God was clear-cut and specifically spelled out. Angelic, holy spirituality in one corner; animalistic, basely human experience in another. Any doubts or questions, any flights of imagination applied to reuniting our spirituality and humanness were strictly taboo, spiritually incorrect.

Needless to say, at the young age of eight, something inside of me closed and I became emotionally absent to those times spent in Sunday School class. And I continued watching PBS.

During the last few months of the Buddha's life, the great teacher was asked by worried students who they should follow after his death. Who was to be their next teacher, their next guide along the spiritual path? The Buddha's response was from his heart. He said, "Be a light unto yourself." It is the very same wisdom Jesus taught, five hundred years later, when He admonished His disciples not to look for the Sacred "Lo here!," or "Lo there! for, behold, the kingdom of God is within you." I believe this wisdom is directing us to acknowledge and cultivate an authentic uniqueness—what we might call a *sacred individuality*—that is innate, particular, and "within" each of us. This teaching directs us to pay attention to our innermost desires, feelings, thoughts, impulses, passions, idiosyncrasies, yearnings, and so forth— and to be honest about them. It asks us not to accept doctrine blindly, but to find out for ourselves, to experience the truth of a teaching for ourselves.

Regardless of religious affiliation, race, gender, or sexual orientation, the wisdom of scared individuality is also one of the most common refrains I've heard while working with those who are terminally ill. Sometimes it is said with a wry smile of larger understanding, almost as if privy to a vast cosmic joke. Sometimes it is said with deep regret and bitterness. Either way the teaching, the message from the bigger picture at life's end, seems to be the same: "If I could do it all over again, I'd not be as concerned about what other people thought. Instead, I'd do more of the things that I really enjoyed. I'd take more risks, be more unique. More myself." A profound yet simple teaching, this wisdom is about being true to yourself and how that trueness is a spiritual practice we can invite into our daily lives and our religious traditions.

In Here, Broadly Conceived

As long as I can remember, the unspoken rule was: If your personality doesn't fit the basic model of your spiritual or cultural tradition, your path is clear. Change your personality. For years I thought the game of life, socially as well as spiritually, was to figure out the way, the style, the pattern of someone else who knew—say, an enlightened person—and follow his or her way. For me, like most of us, the Way to the Sacred seemed to lie elsewhere, outside of my own inner kingdom, light, self, and experience. Outside. Out there.

But, if you recall, in the "Story in Lieu of an Epigraph" my patient Jim who was dying of AIDS in Parkland Memorial Hospital reminds us that the message from that bigger perspective at life's end seems to be what the great teachers have said all along. Become a light unto yourself, seek within. Inside. In here.

But what does this teaching to seek within really mean? Surely our great spiritual teachers are not asking us to make some kind of move toward radical introversion, a kind of spiritual narcissism that ignores the world and other people living around us. Surely we can't all cloister ourselves in a monastery like Thomas Merton, or upon a private lake like Thoreau. What about the rest of us? What does "seek within" mean for the contemporary seeker who lives in today's multicultural, multitasking, busy, busy world?

Well, another translation of that famous line from Luke (17:20–21), a translation that most Biblical scholars prefer nowadays, has Jesus saying: "the kingdom of God is *among* you." For me, this poses no complication or problem to the concept of a teaching that advocates seeking within for wisdom. Actually, I think it helps us tremendously.

The kingdom of God is within/among you.

I see the translation of "among you" as expanding the nature of what we consider to be the "within" of our lives in the first place. In this manner, to seek "within" means not only to seek within your own mind and heart, but to also seek within and "among" the largeness of *your whole life experience*. Imagine how large the landscape for seeking becomes in such a broadly conceived and inclusive notion of the within.

From this broad viewpoint, to seek within is to seek within/among our relationships, within/among our life's triumphs and failures, within/among our loves and losses—within/among *all* of human life experience. Here, seeking opens the wide door of including all that's among and within our moment-to-moment experience of life itself. Infinite, spacious, and unrestrictive.

*   *   *

A reporter once asked Mother Teresa what it felt like to be called a living saint. The nun replied: "Holiness is not just for a few people. It's for everyone, including you, sir." The quality of sacred individuality reminds us of just this truth—that it is your responsibility to explore and cultivate the sacred within your particular human life, a life marked by a uniqueness in personal character, experience, and expression. A life marked by a one-of-a-kind soul. This truth also suggests a radical possibility: that the sacred, as expressed by humanity, can be as diverse and multifaceted as we are as individuals.

And this is what I love so about the teaching of sacred individuality. It has become precious to me beyond words. There is a grand permission, a majestic tolerance and emphasis toward being true to yourself and to others. There is a basic trust in who we are as human beings and the unique gifts we each have to offer. I think back to that weekday morning, while doing my rounds upon the ninth floor in the Infectious Diseases Unit at Parkland Memorial Hospital in Dallas, Texas. I think back now to Jim, the man dying of AIDS, and his intimate deathbed teaching to me. A gift of perennial wisdom. Like Buddha's deathbed teaching that we must be a light unto ourselves, or Jesus' admonition that the kingdom of God is to be found within us, I hear Jim's words to me . . .

"I just want you to know if I could do it all over again, I'd be more outrageous. You know, give 'em more hell. Be more myself and less what everybody said I'm supposed to be. . . . More myself," he repeated softly. *"More myself."*

2

Grand Permission

The teaching to "seek within" promotes a way of courageous self-honesty—especially when social or religious pressures to "keep up appearances" encourage us to pretend otherwise. Sacred individuality asks us to cultivate open-mindedness, tolerance, and a sense of grand permission in our lives and seeking.

AS THE CHINESE TRANSLATION OF MY FIRST BOOK, *Living Our Dying,* was being prepared for publication, the Taiwanese editors asked if I'd write a brief, second preface especially for that edition. Specifically, they wanted to know more about my personal story and spiritual journey since the book's publication in English. Was I still at Parkland Memorial Hospital? Had my views on "conscious dying" changed or evolved? And just what was the emphasis in my spiritual life today? As I wrote the new preface, updating my whereabouts and current work, one question seemed to linger, avoiding a quick response—so, where was I in my spiritual life today? Like many HIV+ people, I'd begun taking the new "cocktail" of protease inhibitors and antiviral drugs. And like many, my immune system was growing stronger, the amount of active virus detectable in my blood had dropped considerably. A significant reprieve from my dying seemed—and still seems, as of this writing—to be at hand.

Yes, a reprieve . . .

For just how long we don't know, but compared to the month-to-month game of waiting, a game many of us in the HIV community had grown accustomed to, this has truly been a significant pause in the process. I remember how a friend of mine once referred to her experience with a life-threatening illness as her "cancer high." She still speaks of the loss she's felt since her recovery. I think many of us long-term survivors understand what she means; we've experienced how the "high" of dying sometimes elevates us beyond our mere humanity. No longer simply an ensemble player, we'd been cast in the leading role of our social circle's great drama—and we also felt a leading-edge excitement of spiritual deepening that accompanies serious illness. The new problem within our medicine-induced reprieve has been the interruption of that spiritual high.

If I'm honest, I must confess how I've felt a loss of the specialness I once so secretly coveted. Yes, my dying is still ongoing, still there; but not so much *here*. It's a time off, a distance away. And I recognize that, for the immediate time, I've lost my star status and center-stage spotlight. Demoted from my exalted position of *Noble Example of Humanity Who Embraces His Dying,* I've become "merely" human again.

I also recognize this is a good thing. The realization I've

had during this "interruption" offers an opportunity for me to practice a much larger sense of permission in my life by being even more honest, more intimate with myself—and with others. I can admit that, yes, I'm often the Great Hypocrite when it comes to "living my dying" or "embracing" my own mortality. I'm often a spiritual mess, despite all my conscious growth and serious seeking.

I'm thinking now about that story of Zen master Suzuki Roshi's dying—the one told in Natalie Goldberg's wise little book, *Writing Down the Bones*. Goldberg writes:

> He died of cancer in 1971. When Zen masters die we like to think they will say something very inspiring as they are about to bite the Big Emptiness, something like "Hi-ho Silver!" or "Remember to wake up" or "Life is everlasting." Right before Suzuki Roshi's death, Katagiri Roshi, an old friend, visited him. Katagiri stood by the bedside; Suzuki looked up and said, "I don't want to die." That simple. He was who he was and said plainly what he felt in the moment. Katagiri bowed. "Thank you for your great effort."

From a strict Zen letter-of-the-law reading, one might say, "How *attached* Roshi is to life, what poor Buddhist form!" But I believe the heart of Buddha smiles widely and, along with us, breathes a good, long sigh of relief at Suzuki Roshi's honesty to his old friend.

Now, if you are at all like me, you've probably experienced various degrees of pressure to "keep up appearances" when it comes to the spiritual path. In spiritual circles, as in most of life, the seeker is often inundated by notions of propriety, ideals that dictate just what is (and definitely what isn't) the appropriately "spiritual" way to react or respond in a given circumstance. We substitute an unquestioned doctrinal correctness for truthfulness of heart. But what if we kept in mind the more honest model demonstrated in this story? What if we kept in mind the courageous (and outrageous) honesty of Suzuki Roshi when he said on his deathbed, "I do not want to die?" He didn't fake it, not even for spiritual appearances. This sincere teacher knew of a higher truth than appearances, an honesty to this very moment of experience. No spiritually correct costume to wear, only an injunction to try to be as self-honest as possible. He reminds us that, again, spiritual depth and maturation are not about outer appearance, but inner awareness.

That is freedom, true liberation—if you ask me.

As I reflect back over my journey, its breadth, its contradictions, misunderstandings, and wonderful, fearful humanity, this is what I've come to believe: *The single greatest lesson I've continued to encounter has to do with permission. It is so important that we give ourselves permission to be fully human, which includes acknowledging our fears as well as our triumphs, if we are to honestly traverse life's great path.*

When I wrote this I had already begun working on this book, but I'd not yet come to understand the "practice of permission" that permeates this book—and my personal journey. Like many in my profession, I often write what I need to learn.

I've since come to believe we cannot possibly begin to fully realize our sacred individuality and the ongoing sense of spiritual maturation without this breadth of permission. Permission to make mistakes. Permission to view our journey as always ongoing and evolving. Permission to allow our spiritual process to take its time. Permission to cultivate a larger faith and image of God that honors life's wonderful, fearful human whole.

A Call to Grandness

I also believe it is sometimes necessary to go a bit further, daring to push ourselves into a slightly maverick, outrageous—(or, for some, heretical?)—depth of permission. It's a quality of seeking I like to think of as *grand permission*. Such a breadth of permission is not something we can accomplish offhand or willy-nilly. It takes a sense of determination and even vigilance to uphold. It's *grand*—almost too large, too open-minded, trespassing over the edges of our more conservative psychospiritual boundaries. And though iconoclastic, grand permission is not arrogant, uniformed, nor without awareness. Like the grandness of, say, an Oscar Wilde or Maya Angelou, it consciously challenges us to rethink, reconsider, and re-imagine our notions of life and its full expression. I've since found that to try to live this wisdom isn't easy. To live this degree of individuality in today's world of conformity and conventionality takes a deep commitment to one's own personal truth and spiritual process.

Throughout the years, I have come to believe that each person is endowed with a one-of-a-kind personality and expressiveness that life needs, that each of us was born to manifest a particular and unique glory unto God and life. Again, to my way of seeing, this is part of what Jesus was hinting at when he said we were to do "greater works" for humankind. Though we are often taught otherwise by a culture that sometimes encourages smallness and conformity, the truth is, you can offer yourself and others a profound and healing sense of grand permission.

In this spirit, you might try seeking out peers or mentors who consciously cultivate the quality of grand permission in their lives and teachings. At first glance, these fellow seekers may not be "doing the spirituality thing." They'll come from all walks of life, all of them creative in their own way, each probably a bit of a rebel, too (though they may have learned to camouflage themselves well). In my experience, if you start to cultivate the quality of grand permission in your own life exploration, you'll soon meet others who'll offer that permission in return. This is one of the ways that authentic spiritual friends gather, and that genuine spiritual community is formed.

Remember, we have been given a sacred individuality by

God so we might express our inner brilliance within this mortal coil. The message from within is, you *can* be grand.

※

A BRIEF POSTSCRIPT: IT'S MY HOPE THAT THROUGH THE STORIES in this book you'll meet all kinds of people—different, distinct, outrageously individualistic, and courageous people— who will not only champion your own personal awareness of grand permission but will also share with you the wisdom and teachings they've shared with me. For me, these stories reaffirm the truth that powerful teachings are often right here before us, and that guidance toward honesty of heart and spiritual depth is found not only upon the pulpit or within scriptures, but also within our own everyday experience and lives. In short, I believe a tangible, almost visceral wisdom is being taught all around us, everywhere we look. It is, in truth, ever-present. Our problem is we just don't recognize it. The spiritual masters have all asked, in their own way, "If not here and now, where else will you find the whole life?" It's here, right before you, within and among the experience of your life, now. That's why the cultivation of grand permission is so important: How else are we to recognize these "everyday" teachings?

3

Daring to Be Spiritually Incorrect

A rigid adherence to simplistic ideals—regardless of religious tradition—usually starves the soul of its individuality and innate wisdom. When it is our authentic calling and way, we must dare to be spiritually incorrect.

THE NEXT PERSON IN LINE HANDED ME A BOOK TO SIGN. "I'm dying," she said plainly. "A kind of leukemia." Then this woman, who looked at most to be in her early sixties, told me her story. She told how, over the past year, her medical treatments failed. How, for three months now, she'd been waiting for the disease to return with vigor, which the doctors promised it would. So she was waiting to die, she said. It was only by accident that she'd read about my book signing in the newspaper.

She nodded to the book she'd just handed me. "I was hoping to find some way to get my oldest daughter to understand what I'm going through. None of my family will talk about my dying. I can sort of understand. I know it scares them." She looked me square in the eyes, her mood shifting as if she were pricked by a sharp pin. "But I'll tell you what really burns me up, because *they* should know better. And that's whenever I mention my leukemia at our Bible study group. The first time I told them that the chemo failed, they said, 'Well, I don't know about you, but *my* God is a God of miracles!' And that's what they still say whenever I bring it up. '*My* God is a God of miracles.' "

"I bet that hurts," I said.

"Yes." She paused and considered. "It did at first. But, you know, it wasn't long before I began to feel sorry for them. You see, they really can't see all the miracles that have happened to me. They really don't understand. I try to explain, but they just can't see it. I've experienced so many, many miracles during this illness. Too many to even count. Why do people think a miracle always has to mean getting cured?"

She whispered confidentially, "You know, I've already outlived my diagnosis by one month. So last week I decided I'd better stop waiting around to die and have some real fun in the meantime. I'm planning a vacation. Next month I'm going to the Bahamas, then to Chicago the month after that, then to Colorado after that. No one understands. They all think I'm crazy. But I'm not. If I die even before the first vacation happens, at least I've had the joy—and it *is* joy— of planning the trips for myself. It's one of the miracles in my life right now. And it's just as big a miracle to me as anything ever has been. I've always wanted to travel and never let myself."

I said, "Well, those are definitely real miracles as far as I'm concerned. And I hope your daughter reads the book and it helps. What's her name?" I lifted my pen, ready to endorse the book.

Then this beautiful woman paused, a slow, wide smile spreading across her lips. "Go ahead and make it out to me," she said. "To Lucille."

Airplane reading, perhaps?

The Narrow View

Lucille's story epitomizes the trap of what I like to call "spiritual correctness." Her support group was so blinded by their own fears and rigid adherence to what they imagined as proper spiritual doctrine, they couldn't see the larger lesson of grace personified right before them. I don't doubt that her friends thought they were being supportive, guiding her back to the correct spiritual perspective. But the reality is that, instead of providing spiritual comfort, support, and empathy, Lucille's Bible group added to her pain by shaming her *for being truthful,* for daring to introduce some "human" honesty into their "spiritual" setting. It's an all-too-common trap. Most of us will experience this kind of ideological arrogance and narrow-mindedness along our pilgrimage (from others, and from within ourselves). Its simplistic black-and-white appeal is one of the great traps for seekers of any religion. At some point, we all fall for it. For a time.

You can hear undertones of spiritual correctness in every religious tradition, even the most progressive: from Judaism and Buddhism, to mainstream Christianity, to the "positive thinking" bent of New Age beliefs. Of course, it's more obvious in certain fundamentalist approaches but, again, the trap of spiritual correctness can find its way into the most seemingly "progressive" pulpits and teachings. Sometimes our need for existential certainty is so desperate, we fool ourselves and inadverntently adopt a bit of spiritual teaching—no matter how open-minded or well-intentioned—in a narrow, zealous way. As honest seekers, it becomes our responsibility to keep check on our own narrow views, and to reconize this kind of spiritual closed-mindedness when it arises in ourselves. Yet the trap of spiritual correctness is not always so obvious as a Bible study group's refusal to hear about one of its member's real-life pain. It can and does often arise in far more subtle ways. An example of this more subtle trickery:

A friend of mine who works with dying children tells a story about her meditation group (which also serves as a kind of caregiver's support group). As she tells it, her group has just concluded their weekly gathering when the meditation teacher turns to her and says aloud, in front of everyone present, "Beth, I really don't know how you do it. You always seem so joyful. You show perfect peacefulness and no fear, yet you work with such pain and suffering. You are a real inspiration. If only we could all be that courageous."

That's the story—so simple and, seemingly, innocent. And, what a nice bit of recognition and acknowledgment for Beth. Or so it seems, at first.

Upon a more thoughtful consideration, we can also see how the teacher in this situation has inadvertently established a model of spiritual correctness that, in practice, denies the true ebb and flow of his students' real lives. After pressing, Beth readily admits that, when she doesn't live up to this model of "perfect peacefulness and no fear," she feels as if she's a "spiritual failure," a "phony" who's good at putting on airs of serenity (her words). She's become trapped in a belief that one must be the "inspiration" at all costs, and that a constant show of "joy" and "positive spirit" is the optimum way toward the Sacred. Life's wonderful emotions are praised as spiritually beneficent, while our fearful emotions are subtly, if not outright, vilified. The "spiritual life" becomes a pristine endeavor to be kept apart from the chaotic mess of real life. It's the common tenor to just about every form of spiritual correctness: a denial of life's grays bolstered by an idealistic, black-and-white interpretation of doctrine.

Thankfully, as we mature within our spirituality, we naturally begin to seek out a more spacious vision of the Sacred. The narrow view of spiritual correctness begins to become less comforting. We need something more. A largeness of vision that, as the beautiful woman at my book signing taught, may include and even celebrate the miracles that occur even when one's cancer does not go into remission. A largeness of vision that calls for honesty, courage, and determination.

Some Pretty Good Company

"It is God's nature to be without a nature." So said the Dominican monk, Meister Eckhart, in his own declaration that we cannot humanly define the limits of the sacred. By the end of his life, the Vatican had charged him with heresy. Now, seven centuries later, Eckhart is considered by scholars and seekers alike to be one of the greatest mystics within the whole of Christian tradition; yet during his own life, he continually kept his church and religion astir because of his often blunt, spiritually incorrect pronouncements. We see this time and time again, regardless of a seeker's religious orientation: The individualistic imagination of the brilliant soul usually annoys the rather dull, hallowed halls of The Established Way. From Jesus, who was branded a heretic and troublemaker for his teachings that went against official Jewish law, to the twentieth century's J. Krishnamurti, who irritated thousands of Theosophical followers by dissolving and renouncing the spiritual hierarchy that had organized around him, the history of our world's religions is filled with saints and seekers who, for following the inner wisdom of their own sacred individuality, were ridiculed as spiritually incorrect for their time.

One of my favorite stories in this genre is about a wealthy young man who apparently has it all, but because of a growing social consciousness, cannot continue to ignore the great poverty and pain within the larger community around him. His emotional state is what we might describe today as a spiritual crisis: He can't understand why life is so painful, inequitable, unjust, and filled with such suffering. (If you recognize the story, please bear with me.) And so the young man begins his conscious spiritual odyssey. By "conscious" I mean that he consciously chooses to envision himself as upon a spiritual journey; he becomes aware that his human life includes something deeper, a spiritual dimension, and he must seek it out more fully. For years the young man zealously follows the religious traditions and practices of his day, renouncing certain foods and pleasures, putting himself through various kinds of rigorous and painful ascetic ordeals. Eventually, even though he becomes quite a local spiritual celebrity with a few followers of his own, he also recognizes that his initial crisis of heart remains. After years of dedicated seeking, he still feels no true inner peace, no authentic understanding nor acceptance of life. It is then, as the story goes, he gives up. He stops the strict adherence to the various spiritual practices he has learned and sits himself down to reflect. Sitting, he remembers how, as a child, he used to sit under a rose apple tree in his father's garden. He remembers how whole and at peace he felt in that childlike state, sitting beneath the tree. He recognizes that he'd already experienced inner peace and acceptance in his life—while sitting as a child. This new practice of sitting, childlike, awake to the whole present moment, becomes the seeker's new way. For the spiritual weakness of giving up his former practices, his students ridicule and then abandon him. But he follows true to his inner heart and remains sitting there, quietly, under that Bodhi tree.

This is the Buddha's story, or at least the beginnings of it. He abandoned the ideals of spiritual correctness and sat down, got still, and shut up. I think it's an interesting and valid endeavor to try to figure out his "method." How did he sit? In what posture and for how long? What did he eat? Of course there can be definite benefit in learning from the experience of other seekers before us (and certainly the religion he founded teaches sitting meditation as one of its primary disciplines). But I believe it is also of great importance to re-imagine this story in broader terms. The young man that would later become known as the Buddha ultimately chose a path that was, in part, quite spiritually incorrect as viewed by the established tradition of his day. Instead of rigidly adhering to a narrow interpretation of doctrine, he followed the direction of his inner heart, imagination, and intuition. And he dared to let that inner wisdom inform, transform, and deepen his larger spiritual pilgrimage.

In a nutshell, this is an archetype for a seeker's experience when he or she is true to the unique calling of sacred indi-

viduality. We confront our more narrow intellectual precon-
ceptions of just what it means to "be spiritual," confront
the established boundaries of where we are allowed to seek
within our life, and begin, instead, to ask the sometimes
difficult questions arising from the heart—questions that
may prove uncomfortable, not to mention unanswerable.
Questions that often go against the grain of the day's popularized spiritual correctness. The journey of authentic spiritual maturation is filled with such moments of great inner
questioning. It is this book's intent to encourage you to ask
these big questions, the deep questions of authentic seeking.
It is also this book's intent to help you cultivate an "atmo-
sphere of permission" that allows you to listen to the wisdom
within and among you. At its foundation, sacred individuality demands a sense of grand, expansive permission.

If what Meister Eckhart said is true—that it is God's
nature to be without nature—then we must also consider
that the road to God may be without a generalized or prees-
tablished nature as well. That's a wide road. A road ex-
tending far beyond what we think we see now, far beyond
any preconceived ideas of spiritual correctness we could possibly imagine.

Again, the history of our world's religious traditions is
replete with saints, mystics, and visionaries who were ridiculed as spiritually incorrect, if not outright heretical for
their own time. So be forewarned: To cultivate your own

spiritual maturity and courageously seek deeper within may, at times, put you at odds against the idealism of popularized spiritual correctness.

The good news is, you are not alone in this great endeavor. And, historically, you're in some pretty good company.

4

Awe

As we deepen in spirit, we come to recognize that God is too big to contain in theories or formulaic scriptural definitions. Part of our work as seekers along any path is to reclaim the largeness of God's ineffability, to reclaim our own personal sense of awe.

WHEN I THINK OF MY CHILDHOOD IMAGES OF GOD, two distinct pictures arise. One is traditional. Up in Heaven an old man with a long, white beard sits on a cloud. He is looking down at me. One of His hands rests on the Holy Bible (always the King James Version), while the other hand points down a finger in horror . . . at my genitals. Remember Him?

Like the other bearded archetype, Santa Claus, this God also knew when I was good or bad and similarly kept a list (but didn't need to check it twice, because He already knew). So not only was God a spiritual Kris Kringle to whom I petitioned my wants and desires, He knew just *how* bad I'd really been. I was so sure that list of His detailed every sinful act, especially masturbation. It's no wonder many of us, at such young ages, sought to compartmentalize our spirituality from our humanness; it was an effective way of diminishing our guilt for being human (and so sexual) after all.

As I said, that's one image of God I remember. The other is not so traditional. It begins with an old black woman, telling stories . . .

The woman's name, my first spiritual teacher outside my family, was simply "Miss Nancy." I'm ashamed as I write this now that I don't know her full name. My family still refers to her simply as Nancy, nothing more. She was my nanny and our housekeeper and so often I, her "white youngen," would sit upon her lap, listening to her stories and hanging on every word she had to say.

Miss Nancy didn't teach me about matters of Spirit by merely citing theological doctrine or scripture. Mostly she told stories. She offered up images, like the huge east Texas sky when viewed from a large meadow. Like the leaves and flowers budding in spring. Like the danger of water moccasins and stinging scorpions. Life was to be awed, and so was God. He, and God was definitely a "He" for Miss Nancy, had infinite mercy and infinite love. And He *loved* me! Not so He could watch over me, or shame me, or reprimand me—besides, in Miss Nancy's mind I just may have been the sweetest little child ever born. Just as I was her white youngen, I was God's beloved youngen, too. No doubt. *Me.* God loved me individually and specifically. With such a big universe, it was indeed awesome to my mind that God would love me specifically. That He had the time. That He could even find me way down here in Marshall, Texas. But He did. Miss Nancy said so, and I didn't doubt her for an instant.

In so many ways her teachings embodied a largeness of God far beyond that bearded, judgmental old man sitting upon a cloud in Heaven. For Miss Nancy, God was to be relished in the vibrant acts of creation, like the batch of baby toads we once discovered under a clay pot in the flower bed, just after an early morning summer rain. And she also taught me to notice God's destruction and the appearance of death. To her, it was all part of God's grandeur. Hers was a God large enough to contain the paradox of both the wonderful and fearful as part of an ongoing cycle of creation and destruction.

I remember another time when Miss Nancy and I found a dead mockingbird on our back porch, its neck snapped to one side, its beak bloodied from where it collided with the kitchen's sliding glass door. We both looked at the bird, studying its horribly still and silent beauty. I'd never been that close to a bird before, that near. I asked, "Why, Miss Nancy? Why did God do this?"

She shook her small, dark head, with short, kinky, silver-white hair, shook it from side to side. "Just don't know. Can't never know why God does what He does. Sure is sad, though. Such a pretty mockingbird. Sure a sad thing to see."

The Field of Unknowing

In the end, all our philosophizing and theologizing about the vast nature of God implodes back into what the early Christian monks called a "cloud of unknowing," or what the Apostle Paul called a "knowledge that passes human understanding." In Taoism this unknowable nature of God is referred to as the Eternal Tao, the "Eternal Truth that cannot be told of"—or thought of, or conceived of. The Hebrews spell this mysterious God "G-d" to emphasize that it cannot be spoken or represented, only pointed toward. For Native American traditionalists of the Lakota religion, *Wakan Tanka*, their name for God, properly translates into "the Great Mystery." Emphasizing how we can never hold a true image of the Absolute in our grasp, the Sufi aphorism bluntly states, "No man has seen God and lived." And even that seminal intellectual Thomas Aquinas, after putting his considerable mind to the test of explaining how we could speak and conceive of God, finally had to conclude, "we remain joined to Him as to one unknown."

Most of us have been taught to fear the *field of unknowing* that lies between the god of our socio-religious culture and the ineffable God that speaks usually within the faintest whisper of our hearts. About this field, the Sufi poet Rumi wrote,

Out beyond our ideas of wrongdoing and rightdoing,
there is a field. I'll meet you there.

When the soul lies down in that grass,
the world is too full to talk about.
Ideas, language, even the phrase *each other*
doesn't make any sense.

A culture of stale moralism has taught many of us to avoid visiting that field beyond the black-and-white certainty of spiritual do's and don'ts. Part of our work as conscious-seekers along any path is to reclaim the largeness of God's ineffability and to reclaim that field of existence that lies beyond conceptual certainties.

As I look back upon the lessons Miss Nancy taught me, this remains most potent: God is too big to contain in theories or formulaic scriptural definitions; so we look to stories around us—stories from nature, from our human joys, as well as frailties and foibles—and we *recognize* in these God's presence; this recognition is not an intellectual understanding, but a texture of experience that is in some way tactile.

At their mystical cores each of the world's great religious traditions remind us we cannot define God, but we can experience It, feel It. Miss Nancy taught me her own private ways to recognize and experience the vastness of God in daily life. And still, in the midst of this sacred recognition, she also taught me to have an awe for the mystery and to remember that, often, we just can't know why life takes a particular turn.

God bless that woman. With her own slave-descendant

breath, sweet and soulful enough to really embrace God's grandeur and majesty, Miss Nancy breathed an authentic reverence for a larger spiritual life-force into my young white-boy lungs.

God bless that woman and her not knowing. Such a big field of sacred unknowing.

❧

TRY THIS: SPEND SOME TIME CONTEMPLATING THOSE EVENTS, happenings, and relationships in your life that, when you think about them, elicit a feeling of *awe*. One quick way to recall this kind of awe is to consider the seeming randomness of how you met a person who has since become a really close friend, a person who has already been truly important in your life. Perhaps this dear person is your spouse. Or a colleague, mentor, partner, or even spiritual advisor. Consider how random your meeting truly was, how wildly serendipitous. Most likely, just a few months before you first met, both of you had no idea nor suspicion of the other's eventual impact upon your lives. But what happens? As if by luck or fate, perhaps against great odds, you both actually meet. You come together. Out of six billion human bodies milling around upon this planet, you two actually cross each other's path. Imagine it: Just how particular and specific are all the elements of this "chance" meeting? Imagine the perfection that seems as if it must have been designed by some great other—be this God, or fate, or whatever. Consider how "right" all the details were for you to not only meet, but to then, over time, become such important friends. Consider all the very particular circumstances that actually occurred for this growing intimacy to blossom. It's truly awesome indeed. When you think about it. That you found one another. Allow yourself to touch upon this awe. For life. For God. For the whole grand mystery of your journey here.

5

Including It All

This quality reminds us that there are no boundaries to the Sacred. And that our spiritual pilgrimage, like life itself, is a journey through the depths as well as the heights. To travel honestly and openly, we'll need to cultivate the quality of including it all. The grit as well as the grace. All of it.

THE FIRST DEAD BODY I SAW WAS MY FATHER'S COUSIN, Sammy. Sammy was a forty-one-year-old man-child with Down's syndrome who lived decades longer than the doctors said he would. I was twenty when he died. Two years later I saw my grandmother laid out, all dressed up in a pink dress, in her coffin, in the same small viewing room Sammy had been laid in, just off the chapel at Eubank's Funeral Home in Mineola, Texas.

I saw only sanitized death. I hadn't seen the grit of dying yet. Later, after my own diagnosis, I would see dying up close. When I worked on the AIDS ward at Parkland Memorial Hospital in Dallas, Texas, I wouldn't hesitate to hug my patients. I held them in my arms at times, cuddling them. Often it was only a patient's mother and me who weren't wearing masks and gloves.

I kissed them hello on their foreheads, and eventually good-bye. I "logged-in" their bodies on the roster that hung on a rusting hook opposite the walk-in refrigerator in the hospital's basement. One unmarked door along a hospital corridor; a narrow, private hallway inside, lead to a shiny metal icebox door, with an old-fashioned icebox handle. The morgue.

How I hated to go down to the morgue. Secretly, I was so grateful when my shift would end and I knew, that if someone died on my floor, it was no longer my job to log-in the body.

What I despised most, however, was escorting a family member down to that cold metal room. I had to do this several times a month. Awkward. Fumbling. Cold, cold room. Dark inside that refrigerator. One naked light bulb glaring. Looking through toe-tags, praying incessantly to find the right name quickly as the mother, father, brother, daughter, lover, or spouse stood outside in the busy hospital corridor. I made them wait outside until I'd found the right toe-tag and wheeled the gurney out of the icebox.

Yes, I tried to keep them away from the door with the icebox handle, away from that meat-locker smell. But it was futile. Seconds after opening the large metal door, the smell of refrigerated, slightly putrid, slightly floral sweet, rotting flesh would sweep over us like a large wave. I couldn't keep it inside. It ate into my nostril lining and my clothes like cigarette smoke in a crowded bar.

Once, a patient's brother unconsciously followed me into the dim, cold room. For an awkward moment we both fumbled, as if we'd walked in on each other while sitting on the toilet. "Could you wait outside please," I said softly. Looking embarrassed, he stepped back into the hallway. Then I realized I'd forgotten the name. Whose toe was I looking for?

To be sure, smelling dead bodies in Parkland's morgue was not my idea of the "spiritual experience." I wanted to touch that Big Wonderful Transcendent Peace of God. After all, I told myself, this was the *spiritual* path I was traveling, not the worldly. One of my first great lessons of spiritual deepening was to re-imagine what I considered to be the ultimate purpose of spirituality. I'd always thought that spirituality was here to help us *escape* life's fearful, painful, and dark experiences. I honestly believed that once I matured spiritually, the journey to the morgue wouldn't touch me at all. I knew that other chaplains were able to find a sacredness when it came to this aspect of the job. I thought that if I could just somehow jump ahead in my maturation and experience the grace, completely bypassing the grit, I'd be making obvious progress. For me, "successful" spirituality was envisioned as a kind of holy inoculation against life's unpleasantries and ills—and that definitely included the morgue. At the time I didn't realize how universal my experience actually was, and how basic was my misunderstanding about spiritual growth.

Every seeker I know has witnessed firsthand how certain aspects of real-life experience are spiritually taboo to acknowledge or talk about, both the pleasurable (such as sex) and the painful (like depression or anger). In some religious circles you can't honestly say, "I am so jealous" or "I'm pissed off," without being regarded as inadequate or inferior. In such a narrow view, many of the very qualities (dark, dirty, gritty qualities) that define us as human beings are routinely denied a seat at the spiritual banquet table (white, pure, unsoiled). The "spiritual life" becomes a somewhat pristine and separate endeavor to be kept apart, undefiled by the mess of everyday reality. From the varied traditions of mainstream Christianity, Judaism, Hinduism, and Buddhism, to the more esoteric forms in what is lumped together under the wide umbrella of the "New Age," this has been one of the great common misunderstandings for many: *Spiritual maturity is imagined as the exclusively blissful, joyous, and trouble-free life.*

And often this mistaken understanding contends that if we feel any "negative" emotional pain—if we let any circumstance in life make us feel angry or hurt or jealous or fearful or any of that painful human, egoic stuff—we're merely demonstrating our *lack* of spiritual maturity. The assumption is that the truly spiritual person can leap beyond the fearfully human, landing peacefully in the seat of enlightened mind. Tibetan lama Chögyam Trungpa described this basic misunderstanding this way:

> There seem to be two possible approaches here [to spiritual seeking]. One is trying to live up to what we would *like* to be. The other is trying to live what we are. Trying to live up to what we would like to be is like pretending we are a divine being or a realized person, or whatever we might like to call the model. When we realize what is wrong with us, what our weakness is, what our problems and neuroses are, the automatic temptation is to try to act just the opposite, as though we have never heard of such a thing as our being wrong or confused. We tell ourselves: "Think positive! Act as though you're okay." Although we know that something is wrong with us on the level of the actual living situation, on the kitchen-sink level, we regard that as unimportant. "Let's forget those 'evil vibrations,'" we say. "Let's think the other way. Let's pretend to be good."

Often, when the distance between our escape-centered spirituality and our real-life walk becomes too great, we experience a kind of spiritual "crisis." This crisis can take many forms, from mild disillusionment to utter loss of faith. We may even feel betrayed by God, or by our spiritual tradition. But it is important to remember that this disillusionment really arises out of our misunderstanding of the true purpose of spiritually—which, again, is not to guarantee us a blissful life, but a meaningful one. Eventually, as we grow and deepen in spirit, we come to yearn for a spiritual path that does not isolate and ignore life's painful qualities, but instead includes and accepts life's grit as essential to the soul's greater growth and fulfillment. This yearning is an inner call for something more honest and authentic than pat answers or clever formulas promising escape.

In my experience, authentic spiritual maturity has much more to do with acceptance, recognition, and *exploration*, and less to do with avoidance, denial, and *escape*. In a deeper spirituality that acknowledges the often gritty reality of our human life experience, one's emotional pain is most definitely *not* understood as a spiritual error, mistake, or lacking—to the contrary. In a maturing spirituality, we begin making room for the possibility that pain and other fearful emotions may sometimes be the manner in which the sacred is speaking to us, revealing its wisdom.

Emotional Pain: A Call to Explore Deeper

A potent analogy can be found when we look at physical pain and its "teaching." We don't doubt that physical pain is often the means by which our body warns us—teaches us—about a problem needing some medical attention. We commonly recognize how physical pain is a "symptom" that often communicates important insight into our present life situation. No less is true with many of our emotional aches and pains. For example, the emotional pain of loneliness can be a symptom calling a person to reach out and connect with other people, to deepen compassion, love, and community. Or the emotional pain and difficulty we're experiencing in a relationship can inspire us to confront specific aspects of our own personality we wouldn't otherwise face—say, a person's jealousy so interferes with his marriage that either he is going to get some professional help in working through his jealousy issues or lose the marriage; only his love for his wife and their partnership could force him to seek out therapy and confront this neurotic jealousy he'd managed to live with otherwise. From a psychospiritual point of view, this kind of self-confrontational insight and growth is one of the primary purposes of intimate relationships. In this scenario, pain is not an error to be dismissed nor escaped, but a calling to explore deeper.

And another compelling reason for us not to deny our emotional pain is that it's often through pain that we recognize injustice. Perhaps we empathize with the pain of a co-worker who is being discriminated against and feel ethically bound to take action. Or we feel the pain of someone's intolerance when it is directed toward us, and because of this pain we begin a self-examination, questioning our own prejudices against others. In each of these examples, emotional pain may offer wisdom, insight, psychospiritual deepening, and sometimes a call to do good. To deny pain is to also risk denying important wisdom. As Rainer Maria Rilke reminds us in his

Letters to a Young Poet: "Why do you want to shut out of your life any agitation, any pain, any melancholy, since you really do not know what these states are working upon you?"

The primary lesson here is one of inclusion.

For the seeker, the question is not whether we can successfully shield our spirituality from life's grit. We can't. The real question is: Do we cultivate a vision that gives us permission to acknowledge and include *all* our life experiences, especially those darker moments, within the boundaries of what is considered appropriate territory for spirituality? How wide a road is our path? When we encounter life's painful and unpleasant experiences, do we pause to consider the possible wisdom beneath the suffering?

Wonderfully, Fearfully Made

To remind myself of this larger vision that embraces all our life experience, the darker as well as light, I try to keep in my mind a kind of refrain that originates in Psalm 139: that we're all "wonderfully, fearfully made." Now, I want to be honest with you. I didn't find this flipping through scripture late one night, but in a beautiful little memoir titled *Wonderfully, Fearfully Made,* by Catholic priest Robert L. Arpin. In the book's introduction, Arpin writes:

Psalm 139 could be a spiritual road map of my life and journey. The path was often uncharted and narrow, branching out in different directions that caused me some anxious, fearful moments when I had to choose which way to go. I realize now that I was trying to run away from God and from my true self only to find both where I least expected to, in the deepest, darkest, and most secret places within me. Wonderful and fearful are apt descriptions for God and for me.

I'd recalled Psalm 139 from my own Christian upbringing, but frankly I didn't remember that "wonderfully, fearfully made" part. To me, Psalm 139 was just one psalm amongst many that seemed to praise God, waxing poetic about His omnipotence. So, I'd not taken the time to revisit Psalm 139 until I came across Father Arpin's memoir a few years back.

As with many aspects of my religion-of-origin, I found that when I returned to take another look, from a more spiritually-grounded and adult-minded perspective, there was more to the teaching than I'd remembered. Psalm 139 begins by describing a God who is intensely personal and intimatley aware of our human life: "Oh Lord, you have searched me and you know me. You know me when I sit and when I rise; you perceive my thoughts from afar. You discern my going out and my lying down; you are familiar with all my ways." Also, this ever-present God cannot be escaped, nor shielded from our human reality. The psalmist asks, "Where can I go from your spirit? Where can I flee from your presence? If I go up to the heavens, you are there; if I make my bed in the depths, you are there." Everywhere, within everything, this God knows no boundaries of spiritual correctness. "Even the darkness will not be dark to you . . . for darkness is as light to you."

Here, about halfway into the psalm, I was taken aback by the scripture's broad, encompassing inclusiveness. This God seemed . . . well, different. Not quite that Judgmental Old Man ensconced up there on His cloud in Heaven that I'd come to expect. Then, at verse 14, the distance between the wondrous, holy "light" and the fearful, worldly "darkness" is boldly dissolved, as the psalmist explains, "I praise you because I am fearfully and wonderfully made." *I praise you because I am fearfully . . . made.* After years of trying to avoid life's emotional pain and discomfort, I think many of us are coming to realize that, yes, wonderful and fearful are apt descriptions of our human life journey. Perhaps we are *both* wonderfully and fearfully made. And, yes, perhaps this is intentional.

But, as I read it, Psalm 139 goes even further. It pushes beyond a simple acknowledgment or acceptance of "fear" as legitimate to our spiritual life. Let's face it, the psalmist is unmistakably *grateful*. This is a psalm of praise! "I praise you because I am fearfully and wonderfully made." For those of us in the emergent culture of contemporary spirituality, a profound question arises from the psalmist's effusive and, we might even say, extreme gratitude. Why praise God for being fearfully made? Why thank God for the darker, shadow side of our lives?

This is one of those "big" questions of life. It asks us to journey beneath simplistic definitions that patly label "fear" or fearful emotions as our enemy, as the antithesis of a sacred way. It asks us to seriously consider a great mystery of a maturing authentic spirituality:

Why praise God for the shadow and fearful aspect of my life?

This is also a highly personal question—whose answer lies, I think, more in direct experiential knowing than conceptual theological understanding. It is a question we revisit again and again as we mature along our own conscious deepening. But I would like to offer one hint of a suggestion, here, early on in this book's progression. One of the reasons for why the psalmist *might* be grateful to God, grateful for his own human fearfulness, may have to do with empathy and authentic compassion—with the recognition of heart.

Saint Francis of Assisi told the story of his encounter with a leper on the road and called it his moment of conversion. It seems that despite his faith and zealous charity, the sight of the leper who was disfigured and covered in lesions repulsed and frightened him. He wanted to run away, but he could not move. He felt himself inextricably drawn closer and closer toward the leper. Finally he reached out and embraced the leper. When I first heard this story I assumed that Saint Francis had conquered his fear by seeing Christ in the leper. Now I have come to believe that when he looked at the leper, Saint Francis saw himself.

—Fr. Robert L. Arpin

The quality of *including it all* is about allowing what we, in our doctrinal escapism, have previously defined as "small"— like times of anger, boredom, or frustration—to become part of the larger texture of our spiritual seeking. Zen teachings encourage students to practice what is called "beginner's mind," to have a fresh, open-minded approach to all situations—like a beginner does. The expert already thinks he knows, there's not much room for questioning and mystery; but the beginner is always open, aware. To me it sounds much like what Jesus was saying when He told His students to become like little children. A child is a natural explorer, always open-minded, always inquisitive. Always including it all.

Can we allow our experience of the Sacred to become large enough to see that everything we experience is part of a larger spiritual way? Arguments, housework, sex, shopping, anger, joy—all of it? Can we cultivate a perspective where all of life becomes territory for appropriate spiritual exploration?

I believe a tangible, almost visceral wisdom is being taught around us, every day—and this wisdom is intensely personal, designed and expressed particularly for each person within his or her life. Our problem is we just don't recognize it. Because this teaching doesn't fit into the predetermined ideals of the "Spiritual Experience," we often, like I did in the morgue at Parkland, turn away, closing our minds and separating ourselves from any awareness of this ever-present teaching. Still, the Sacred is there—before us. Jesus taught that the kingdom of God was among us, and to emphasize how intimately present this kingdom was He proclaimed it to be "at hand"—right here, right now. Buddha taught the same; both our suffering and our enlightenment are in this very experience of the here-now. Native American elders taught that "today is a good day to die," reminding themselves and tribal members that each moment should be lived fully, appreciated and honored as if it were your last. The great Hindu spiritual masters repeatedly told their students, "Be here now." Each of these traditions ask, in their own way, "If not here and now, where else will you find the whole life?" It's here, now, right before you, within and among the experience of your wonderfully, fearfully human everyday life.

This is indeed the question a seeker naturally comes to ask, as she or he matures along a chosen path: *How can I realize the Sacred if I'm busy trying to escape the here-now?* A good, cutting-to-the-bone question that encourages us to remember the quality of including it all.

❧

AND, FOR THE RECORD, I STILL DON'T LIKE MORGUES. BUT THE difference now is that I watch myself closely when in such a situation and don't seek to escape my uncomfortable feelings. Instead, I *try* to include them and explore deeper. I *try.* That's the process—trying to go a little deeper, to find what's beneath the emotional discomfort and so discover something about ourselves, or life, or God, if we can. I've since learned that one of the things I didn't like about Parkland's morgue—indeed, most morgues—is the sterile, institutional feel of the space; the body is usually not treated sacredly or with reverence; the life lived seemingly not honored. I learned that another reason why I was so uncomfortable in escorting family members to see the body of a loved one (quite often a man my own age or younger) had a lot to do with my own fear of my parents having to witness my dead body. And so on. And I'm sure there's more to learn, greater depths to explore. More to include.

And so more to love. More to give and to receive. Life is far deeper than any simplistic definitions can offer, and so is its journey. Cultivate the quality of including it all. Become a beginner again. Become like a little child, open-minded and inclusive of the way before you in your life now.

6

Cosmic Irony

There's a lot of joy and humor along the spiritual path—especially those moments when we suddenly get the cosmic irony of just how hilarious we are while playing our ego games. It can become a recognition: "Ah, caught myself there! Just look at me, how full of myself! Yes, the joke's on me . . . Good, caught myself there!"

I REMEMBER AN OCCASION JUST BEFORE THE PUBLICA-tion of my first book. It was decided that I needed to have a sample video for the purpose of promotion, so we put out the word for a hastily arranged lecture that was to occur in a matter of days. Because of my track record in attracting crowds, and because I live in a Mecca of the spiritual/self-improvement scene, Santa Fe, everyone expected that even with such short notice we'd have at least fifty or so people show up. No problem. The evening arrived, and, counting the camera operator and the person who worked the door, we had a grand total of six people present. Seven, if you included me. After a quick meeting, we decided it wouldn't be a total loss if the camera kept a tight, close angle on me, and I simply did the presentation as though I were addressing the larger audience. It was only an hour-long talk, and I'd given it plenty of times before. No problem, I thought again.

Well—the talk was a pure, unadulterated disaster. I tried to fake it for the camera and the original intent (marketing the book), but in order to connect with those present I needed to be much more intimate and less didactic than a lecture-hall style of presentation demanded. Halfway through, I flagged the camera operator and asked her to stop. Right in front of everyone, I put my head in my hands and started to laugh. Then I had to apologize to the audience. I'd been babbling on and on about honesty—about being "awake" and "present" to our moment-to-moment living/dying—for a good twenty minutes before I realized *I* wasn't present at all. I was far away in the fantasy land of a large, full audience, giving my standard stump speech about conscious living and dying. The joke was on me, but it was a juicy opportunity to practice what I was preaching and come back down to real-life earth. We pulled our chairs in a circle, which was much more appropriate for the group's small size, and finished the hour with people from the group sharing their stories, too.

That was joyous. There is a lot of joy, a lot of wonderful humor along the spiritual path. I love those sublime moments when I suddenly get the cosmic irony of a situation. When I realize just how hilarious I am pretending to be somebody I'm not. All of us experience this from time to time. For the seeker, it becomes a kind of game: "Ah, caught myself there. Just look at me, how silly, how full of myself I am today. Yes, the joke's on me. Good, good. Caught myself there."

Of course, recognizing cosmic irony is nothing new. It's particularly evident within our cultural and political institutions in the various forms of the Clown archetype. From early Greek philosophy that described man as the "laughing animal," to the court jester in Medieval times, to the antics of a cinematic Charlie Chaplin fighting the evils of unchecked industrialization, the teaching and lightness of the Clown, and his or her ability to bring communal laughter to a gathering, should not be underestimated. Still, we've pretty much avoided bringing the Clown and its awareness of cosmic humor into our religious ceremonies and imagery.

Here, we could learn a thing or two from the Pueblo cultures in New Mexico, who for centuries have cultivated the ceremonial role of the Clown or jokester in religious ceremonies. The "sacred clowns," commonly known as *kosharis*, continually keep the tribal awareness grounded in the cosmic irony of the moment as they mock the overly righteous or pious tendencies of spiritual life. Kosharis often participate directly within the tribe's ceremonial dances and rituals, poking fun at the shaman and otherwise serious ceremony. Almost nothing is taboo in this expression of cosmic humor, including sexual innuendo. From the native way of seeing, all our human foibles and frailties are legitimate targets for spiritual teasing. The sacred clown's function is to remind all present of their balanced place in the cosmos—both that of serious seeker and that of "laughing animal."

For most of us, however, by far the most delicious stories that demonstrate how susceptible we are to cosmic irony are those stories that come from the dead-on honest innocence of our children. There's a time before a certain age when children don't yet have the capacity to understand the finer subtleties of our social taboos. They simply wish to communicate their truth to those around them, directly and honestly. It is a depth of wisdom to which we adults have long since grown quite unaccustomed.

One of my favorite stories in this genre comes from Anne Lamott's wise little book *Bird by Bird: Some Instructions of Writing and Life.* Her story goes:

> My son, Sam, at three and a half, had these keys to a set of plastic handcuffs, and one morning he intentionally locked himself out of the house. I was sitting on the couch reading the newspaper when I heard him stick his plastic keys into the doorknob and try to open the door. Then I heard him say, "Oh, shit." My whole face widened, like the guy in Edvard Munch's *Scream.* After a moment I got up and opened the front door.
>
> "Honey," I said, "what'd you just say?"
>
> "I said, 'Oh, shit,'" he said.

"But, honey, that's a naughty word. *Both* of us have absolutely got to stop using it. Okay?"

He hung his head for a moment, nodded, and said, "Okay, Mom." Then he leaned forward and said confidentially, "But I'll tell you why I said 'shit.' " I said Okay, and he said, "Because of the fucking keys!"

Here, I refer you back to Psalm 139: "Oh Lord, you have searched me and you know me. . . . Before a word is on my tongue you know it completely, Oh Lord." Oh yes. There is indeed a lot of joy and humor along the spiritual path—especially those moments when we suddenly get the cosmic irony of just how hilarious we human beings can be.

7

Larger Faith

What would it mean to cultivate trust in the larger, inexplicable process of life at work? To cultivate a faith that goes beyond the old-fashioned "certainty of doctrine" model ("I never doubt, I have faith!")? A faith that is large enough to honestly embrace life's experiences of fear and unknowing as legitimate lessons along our spiritual pilgrimage?

THE SUPERVISING CHAPLAIN SAID, "I HAVE A QUESTION for you. A riddle actually." She was addressing the gathering of new intern chaplains, of which I was one. We sat in a small circle, like group therapy, all eight of us, and waited for our supervisor to give us the riddle. After a moment of silence, she asked: "How do you tell a five-year-old child how much God loves her after her mother has just died on the operating table?"

One of the benefits of a Clinical Pastoral Education internship at such a large, metropolitan hospital like Parkland Memorial in Dallas, is that life's "big questions"—what is the meaning of life when it's filled with such suffering; how could a loving God allow this; what does it mean to have faith—are in your face daily. It was this riddle that helped me to begin opening the Pandora's box of spiritual doubt and fear that any serious inquiry into the nature of faith must eventually confront. Thankfully, our chaplaincy program was truly ecumenical and didn't seek to impose doctrinal certainty, but rather to expose experiential process. What we learned usually directed us back to the reality of daily experience, our daily walk. The theory behind Clinical Pastoral Education is that there is no better place to examine how your spiritual talk lives up to your real-life walk than the constant pain- and death-filled environment of a hospital. This riddle—call it a Christian parable or a Zen koan—was used as a teaching tool to remind us chaplains of a larger model for faith itself.

Again, the riddle began with this question: "How do you tell a five-year-old child how much God loves her after her mother has just died on the operating table?"

We each awaited the riddle's answer. Our supervisor's response was direct. "The answer is," she said, "you don't."

How do you tell a five-year-old child how much God loves her after her mother has just died on the operating table?

You don't.

As chaplains at an "interfaith" hospital like Parkland, it was not our job to instruct people about God and Her ways. Rather, we were to listen, to empower, to elicit feelings and to further the patient's emotional/spiritual odyssey when appropriate. We were certainly not to truncate a patient's movement through a natural emotional process like fear or anger (unless it somehow interfered with the medical practitioners' ability to do their job). Ours was not the old-fashioned, heroic model of faith exemplified by the idealized priest from an old Bing Crosby movie, who was continually telling his flock, "Don't worry, just have faith because you're in God's loving hands." Ours was a process-oriented model that engendered faith and trust in a larger, inexplicable life process at work.

Like most seekers beginning their conscious journey into spirituality, I'd accepted an antiquated, narrowly-defined notion of faith without hesitation. In my model of spiritual seeking, faith was usually viewed in terms of strength, fortitude, and heroism—as we progressed in our religious devotion we were supposed to develop a "stronger" faith. A strong faith proclaimed an unwavering doctrinal certainty; to have faith means to never doubt, period. The quality of a *larger faith* is purposefully juxtaposed to that more popularized, heroic sibling who's defined by strength. A larger faith is defined by capacity and size. A larger faith seeks a sense of inclusiveness and tolerance within our spiritual pilgrimage, offering refuge and shelter for those sometimes spiritually incorrect feelings of fear, uncertainty, and doubt. A larger faith acknowledges the darker side of our emotional lives— the grief, anger, and rage, the out of control, irrational, and seemingly purposeless mess of human experience. This faith is a moving emotional force that is big enough to include our times of doubt and unknowing and even disbelieving. And its waters run not only deep, but often rough and dark.

As we begin to re-imagine our model of spiritual maturation to include the wonderfully, fearfully human whole of our experience, most of us find we are likewise re-imagining our concept of faith. This newer, larger faith is not a belief that will somehow usher us "beyond" life's grit, but a belief—a faith—in how grace and grit are all part of one larger process. A larger faith asks us to cultivate all the qualities of spiritual maturity, to offer ourselves and others the grand permission to be fully human, remembering that we often don't have the answers, that we are here to learn and include the entirety of our life experience within a conscious spiritual path.

How do you tell a five-year-old child how much God loves her after her mother has just died on the operating table?

You don't.

❧

TRY WORKING WITH THIS RIDDLE FOR YOURSELF IN DAILY LIFE. Let the riddle's inherent difficulty do its alchemy upon your desire for a smaller faith that offers clear-cut answers and idealistic spiritual certainty.

I've found that floating the riddle within my mind, giving

it another turn, is a potent spiritual practice. The beautiful thing about this riddle is that it changes as you work with it. Just as a bit of scripture from the Bible or a Zen koan, the riddle grows, deepens, and matures as we do.

8

Soft Courage

The old-fashioned, popularized image of courage encourages us to overcome adversity through a kind of tough-guy attitude of strength and fortitude. Its motto might be: Keep a stiff upper lip no matter the difficulty. A kind of "hard" courage that asks us to harden ourselves against frailty, to be tougher than the next person.

"EVERY THREE MONTHS." CATIE REPEATED THE HOLLOW words to herself as a tremor of loss shook through her. Her husband held her like a precious, dried leaf that could break into splinters at the slightest mistouch. Into his chest, she began sobbing for the first time since the surgery. "Every three months they test to see if it's returned."

Theirs was a marriage most spoke of with envy. When you thought of Tom and Catie a secret smile emerged upon your lips, and inside you felt hope because here—at last, it seemed—was a couple who truly loved one another. Their love extended itself in all they did together. Still young, in their late thirties, avid hikers and bicyclists—every spring and summer weekend you could find them camping in Virginia's nearby Blue Ridge Mountains. And, oh, how notorious they were for making love under the moonlit sky on those nights deep in the woods. They relished each other. On so many levels, Tom and Catie were the couple everyone wanted to be: young, healthy, sexy, intelligent, psychologically astute, and wholly committed to one another. It was only weeks before Christmas when Catie could no longer dismiss the pain in her right breast as insignificant. It was not too long into the new year when both of her breasts would be removed in a radical mastectomy, and she would find herself receiving radiation treatments atop the scars and empty space where her breasts once were.

And weeks passed.

He'd only seen her scars once, by accident when he'd walked in on her dressing one morning. Tom knew she felt incomplete, inadequate, no longer all of who she had been— not an uncommon story—and the counselor had forewarned them both. But, still, he sensed that something more than flesh had been extracted by the surgery. A safe passageway between her heart and his seemed to have been cut away as well. Weeks passed.

On a cold March afternoon Catie returned from work to find Tom home early. Logs in the fireplace burned and popped as music from *Bridges of Madison County*—her favorite soundtrack—floated in the air. She smelled one of Tom's famous apples pies. Where did he get the apples this time of year? She knew he preferred fresh, locally grown Virginia apples for his pies. "We've just got to wait 'til next fall," he'd say whenever she'd tease him about wanting an apple pie. "Wait 'til the local apples are in season."

Tom stuck his head into the hall foyer from the kitchen. "Hey, hon. Pie's coming out of the oven now."

Catie just nodded, unsure of the change.

Later, with two plates of finished pie on the coffee table before them, she sipped a large mug of black coffee and sat beside him on the couch. "Thank you," she said softly.

"For what?" Tom asked.

"For this. For the fire and the pie." Then she giggled freely to herself. "I can't believe you made it with apples from California."

Tom smiled. "We all have to adjust to change sometimes."

Her body tightened as if an open sore had been accidentally brushed by his hand.

"I miss you," Tom said carefully. "And I miss touching you. I'm so afraid to talk to you about this. I'm so scared right now I'm shaking."

And as he spoke the words, her hands unconsciously moved to her chest, protecting, covering the scars beneath her blouse.

He continued, "Catie, please help me. I don't want to be afraid to touch you. Tell me what to do."

Catie felt her own hands trembling as they massaged

against the hollows where her breasts once were. A tear streaked down her cheek. "To begin," she said, "I need you to kiss my scars."

One of contemporary culture's most popular archetypes for the Seeker is found in the movie *The Wizard of Oz*. In this modern myth, the Seeker is depicted by the trinity of tin man, scarecrow, and lion—seeking, respectively, a brain (knowledge and understanding), a heart (love, compassion, emotional awareness), and courage. We are accustomed to spiritual seeking emphasizing the way of knowledge and love. But what does it mean to seek spiritual courage?

The kind of courage that a maturing spirituality asks of us is not the old-fashioned, heroic model of courage defined by keeping a stiff upper lip. To the contrary, this courage is exemplified by flexibility, inclusiveness, and softness. As Stephen Levine says, "It's hard to kiss someone when you have a stiff upper lip." This quality of *soft courage* is something far different from the popular, heroic model—more like the gentle Buddhist monk and peace activist Thich Nhat Hanh than Dirty Harry, more like the self-disclosing alcoholic who shares of his relapse at an AA meeting than the fireman who jumps into a raging river to save a child from drowning. More like the husband and wife in the above story: Tom with the courage to say, "Tell me what to do";

and Catie, with her courage to answer, "To begin, I need you to kiss my scars." An honest, soft courage. A courage that opens the heart, reveals vulnerability, and trusts in a larger process at work.

Make no mistake about it, being true to yourself and your unique individuality demands the quality of soft courage. It takes courage to step out of the safe, convenient, and comfortable boundaries we've established for our lives; courage to give ourselves a wider (and so, potentially, a more confrontational) landscape in which to seek and explore; courage to give up the illusion that we will one day get "everything right"; and courage to honor and appreciate the divine/human mystery that is ultimately beyond our conceptual understanding altogether. It takes courage to kiss our scars, figuratively as well as literally.

I've witnessed seekers muster that depth of individualistic, soft courage many times—especially when confronted with their own impending death. An authentic awakening to mortality can have profound ramifications to your life and how you choose to live it. This is one of the great blessings and initiations that our dying friends and loved ones often bestow; they challenge us to become more fully ourselves *now*, before we are upon our own deathbeds, realizing a life—and paradise—lost. They challenge us to truly experience our lives and become what American Zen teacher Joko Beck refers to as a "larger container" of life itself. We are each called upon to become larger containers of life's full experience, to kiss our scars and the scars of those we love.

The Heart's Armor

In that old-fashioned model of courage, our response is usually to harden ourselves by hardening the armor around our hearts. It is a mode of self-protection and survival everyone understands because we've all armored our hearts to differing degrees. This armoring is usually constructed of suppressed emotions, denied pains and memories, the unfinished business of personal grievances and anger. Some of this heart armoring is thin and easy to strip away, while the other is seemingly impervious. In certain circles, we've even come to sport our armored hearts like heroic, battle-won medals. We point to athletes, warriors, and successful financiers, admiring how "tough-hearted" they are when it comes to getting the job done. Of course, much of this represents a popular culture out of balance, with upside-down priorities that value the commercial over the spiritual and emotional life. A maturing spirituality recognizes the necessity of getting beyond such ego games and down to the tender heart that beats beneath our leathered armor. We can recognize the false glorification of such armor—hard courage—for what it is: a variation on the theme of that "basic misunderstanding" where the stiff upper lip of social or spiritual correctness is mistakenly valued over truth and honesty to your real-life experience.

As we work to dissolve the layers of defensiveness we've erected around our heart, usually we begin to experience the emotionally painful process of this disarmoring. Most of us who have done any kind of therapy are familiar with this dynamic—the deeper we go, the more painful are the wounds we experience. As we let go of our armor and defensiveness, we may have to face our own inadequacies and feelings of guilt. Or, we may have to again experience a long-buried pain that another, perhaps a parent or guardian, once inflicted upon us. Almost always the process of disarmoring, of healing into the softer heart, involves some degree of emotional pain—some anger, doubt, grief, or fear. so it is important to understand that uncomfortable emotions will naturally arise as we work to let go of our armor. This is the process of true emotional healing. Here each person must allow their disarmoring process to take the time it needs. Through spiritual and psychological practices, you can consciously work to soften and dissolve your heart's armor, but ultimately one cannot bypass the pain of the disarmoring process. We have to kiss our scars, remain attentive, consciously following our pain through its process. Yes, we can evoke and facilitate our heart's softening. But we can't fake it, and insist—with the hardness of certainty—that our armor be magically gone. Authentic spiritual maturation takes soft courage and endurance.

Softening Heart, Softening Belly

This metaphor of hardening and softening comes from the conscious living/dying work of Stephen and Ondrea Levine. Their work has been immensely valuable to me in my own process—not just because their methods provide an accurate way to imagine our psychospiritual work and process, but because it offers a simple, profound practice to breakthrough this hardening. The Levines call this practice "softening the belly." They view the heart and belly as inextricably related: The emotional armoring around one's heart manifests itself physically into a kind of "hardness" in the belly. In short, your heart's armor causes a hardness in the belly. But the relationship, they find, is causal in both directions. When the belly becomes rigid, you can consciously work on softening the belly and that, in turn, will soften the armoring around the heart. So "softening your belly" is a practice that helps expand access to your heart. Armored heart, hard belly. Soft belly, opening heart.

In my experience, this practice of softening the belly when I feel a fearful tightness has been a powerful way to cultivate a more conscious, inclusive, and mature spiritual awareness.

It is a nondenominational advisor that never lies: when my belly is hard, time to soften. One of the primary benefits of this practice is its *immediacy*. It can be done anywhere at any time. Also, the practice is fairly straightforward and self-explanatory. To begin with, just try the practice as you read these words:

> *Take a moment and become aware of your body. Focus your attention on your belly. Is this part of your body tight? Usually, the answer will be, "Yes, my belly is tight." Next, become aware of your breath, your breathing in and out. As you focus on your breathing—in and out, in and out—also bring your awareness to your tight belly. As you exhale, breathing out, try to soften your belly a bit. Breathing out, softening belly. Breathing out, letting go of tightness. Each time you breathe out, soften your belly again. You might like to imagine the Buddha's big belly, pliable, relaxed, flabby—the very opposite of our culture's chiseled, tight abdomen of heroic perfection. Or, for a Christian image, think of Mary's large, soft belly, pregnant with the Christ child. Find an image that works for you, and breathe into your soft belly. Letting go. Breathing out, softening belly. Letting it all hang out. Breathing out, softening. Feeling it.*

That's the practice. It's that simple and accessible.

Like other psychospiritual practices, softening the belly becomes easier the more you do it. This softening certainly need not be reserved for special, crisis situations. If you're at all like me, the more you become aware of yourself and your body, you'll also come to recognize how the belly lives in an almost constant state of tightness. Over the years most of us have stored up layers and layers of armoring around our hearts, which are also layers of tightness in our bellies.

So there is much softening to be done. And, without hesitation, softening the belly is one of the most profound means I know to cultivate and explore soft courage.

Softening, softening . . .

9

Ongoing Evolution

In any given religious tradition, at any given time, doctrinal belief is constantly being re-examined, re-explored, and re-questioned in light of contemporary, real-life experience. Still, many of us have become lazy and let our spiritual advisors do all the questioning for us. Why not participate in the questioning for ourselves, as well?

THE RETIRED MINISTER JUST SHOOK HIS HEAD. He didn't need to sigh, I could feel his exasperation. A group of us were well into a week-long workshop on "Sacred Individuality" at Ghost Ranch Conference Center near Abiquiu, New Mexico. It was shortly after the conclusion of the morning session, and the minister and I were standing on the portal outside our group's meeting room.

"What's on your mind? Trouble with all this emphasis on seeking within?" I asked.

"Well," the man replied. "Some."

Towering in the distance were those stunning pink-red, sandy-colored cliffs that Georgia O'Keeffe made so famous through her paintings. No place better to talk about God and Spirit than Ghost Ranch, I promise.

The retired minister continued, "When you encourage us to seek within, well, it's nice enough sounding. But it doesn't leave much room for following scripture. What about studying scripture and trying to live in accordance? I'd imagine that scripture is a 'without' teaching as far as you're concerned. I know you try to honor everyone's different religious beliefs; you've made that clear enough. And as far as I know every religion has scripture of some kind. But you don't seem to take it too seriously; and for me, as a Christian, I do take my scripture seriously. I guess I need to understand where scripture meets with this idea of seeking within."

It's a crucial question: Where does seeking within/among your own life experience intersect with established religious doctrine and scripture?

Often, when I talk to a group of people I know to be mostly of a certain faith (say, when I'm speaking at a particular church or group), I can tailor my talk to speak best to a chosen tradition. Though Ghost Ranch is a retreat center run by the Presbyterian Church USA, its attendees are usually quite diverse (for example, only about half present at this particular workshop self-identified as Christians). Because of this diversity, the tone of the workshop—like this book—was purposefully interfaith in presentation. I'd use Jesus' words here, Buddha's there, with nice sprinkling of various other traditions throughout . . . Hindu, Hebrew, Sufi, Native American. And so I wasn't surprised by this man's concern: He'd come to a Protestant-organized retreat center, was a retired Protestant minister, signed up for a workshop on spirituality, and we'd hardly referred to traditional Christian scripture at all (in fact, I'd quoted the Bible only once so far: that quote of Jesus from Luke about seeking "within/ among you"). He was used to approaching spirituality from the outside-in, starting from scripture then relating the teaching to his mind-heart. In our workshop, we were taking the opposite path. Assuming that most of those present had already spent considerable effort approaching their spirituality from the outside (that is how you learn about your tradition's teaching and history, after all), in this workshop we were trying the opposing tact. We began by giving ourselves permission to approach spirituality from inside-out, from the primacy of one's personal experience in relation to the historical teachings of a particular tradition or doctrine. We certainly weren't advocating that anyone throw the baby of established religious tradition out the window with the more doctrine-glorifying bathwater; but we were asking ourselves to let imagination—sometimes wild, sometimes outrageous— enter into how we approached our spirituality in the first place. From this retired minister's perspective, you always began (and ended) with the authority of scripture, *period*. Our emphasis upon this individualized "within" teaching seemed nothing less than a confrontation to his very way of seeking.

Again, the question is: Where does the teaching to "seek within" and doctrine of established tradition/scripture meet?

The best answer I've come to is these meet in yourself, within your heart and mind, within and among your whole life experience. Honestly letting scripture (or whatever teaching you follow) "meet" within your heart and mind, within your life, is the transformational challenge for all seekers— both the person committed exclusively to one specific path, like this minister, as well as the seeker who approaches spirituality in less traditionally defined ways. And it is also necessary to note that this "meeting" is not always a pleasant experience. It asks us to take a certain degree of responsibility that many of us would rather turn over to others—to our teachers, elders, and spiritual advisors.

A sincere seeker will need to cultivate the permission to say to his or her spiritual advisor, "You know I just don't get it. This teaching just doesn't ring true for me. Let's talk about this, explore it together." I believe the inquisitive, individualist seeker is the type of student all good spiritual advisors truly cherish. Why? Because a good teacher recognizes your authentic sincerity in searching for truth and becomes excited; he or she recognizes in you a conscious fellow traveler along the path, a sincere pilgrim like themselves. In short, an authentic teacher will re-experience the joy and importance of true seeking when they have an authentic student; it's what all good teachers (of any disciple) live for. So if your spiritual advisor doesn't honor your sincere questioning and exploration, doesn't encourage it (and I'd even go as far as to say if he or she isn't excited about your work with them), my advice is to find another spiritual advisor.

In your tradition of seeking, are you encouraged to voice your true feelings and/or uncertainties as you grow in spirit? Are you allowed to explore theology for yourself, or are such questionings to be left entirely to the "professionals"—that's regardless of tradition: a priest or rabbi, a shaman or therapist? Does your spiritual tradition consider itself to be continually evolving—at least as far as the way we human beings practice and understand it? For me, these are vital questions.

At my workshops I remind the participants that, historically, there have been many Christians who said, "Nope, I don't get it," to the Bible when scripture was used to justify slavery, or the repression of women, or the Holocaust, and so forth (up to the hottest topic of our day, the ordination and/or marriage of gays and lesbians). Some Christians who disagree with their denomination's official reading of scripture reason that the particular scripture is misinterpreted and twisted, while others reason that certain aspects of scripture are culturally dated and not relevant to today's worldview. (At any theological seminary there are shelves of books on just this subject, the difference between Biblical "practice" on the one hand—what is practiced by the cultures reported in the Bible, like slavery and submission of women to men—and Biblical "principle" on the other— what the heart or spirit of scripture as a whole is believed to intend.) The same kind of debate flourishes in most religious traditions. For example, Buddhists regularly disagree over just how liberally or conservatively, literally or metaphorically, one should approach the Basic Precepts—a scriptural core of Buddha's teaching.

My point in all this is that, within any given religious tradition, at any given time, doctrinal belief is constantly being re-examined, re-explored, and re-questioned in light of contemporary, real-life experience. The reality is, our theological understanding is always growing and changing to some degree. Sometimes this growth is drastic. Other times, subtle. Spiritual understanding, both on the personal level of the individual and the communal level of organized religion, is part of an *ongoing evolution*. (Now, there's some cosmic irony.)

Our problem is, as seekers, many of us have become lazy and let our theologians or spiritual advisors do all the questioning for us. I believe a mature spirituality encourages personal participation. It asks each seeker to hold his spiritual "talk" up to the mirror of his real-life "walk" of personal experience. We must personally participate in the ongoing evolution of our spiritual deepening—and of our chosen religious practice. And so, you and I are encouraged to find the contradictions in our beliefs, to grapple with them, to explore them and dare to think for ourselves. And we are also encouraged to really feel these contradictions. To soften our bellies to them. To live with them for a while and truly seek a deeper understanding that goes beyond the mere words and concepts that doctrine may espouse.

In short, we are asked to seek the spirit of the teaching, to get to the heart of the matter with self-honesty and awareness. We are asked to refuse to accept doctrine blindly without personal exploration. This is the often difficult work that is at the heart of spiritual maturity.

The retired minister and I stood there under Georgia O'Keeffe's mountain. As we talked about the importance of finding the essence of scripture and spiritual teaching, I believe we both came a little closer to something profoundly bigger than our words. I honored his sincerity, and he mine. I'll be honest here, as he first expressed his concerns, I assumed he was probably too fearful to try a looser hold upon his scriptural formulas, but I came to see how that was just my own prejudice and reactivity to some early childhood experiences within the southern Church. Because, as we continued to talk, gently but passionately, we both began to realize that the kingdom of God was among us, here, right now. Among us—among him and myself. We were co-creating the sacred at that very moment as we tried, with openness and sincerity, to touch one another with our hearts and minds. All we had were our words and thoughts and the cool mountain breeze blowing between us, but it was enough. That's how I experienced it anyhow. And I believe he did, too. We ended our conversation, neither really having convinced the other wholly of his view. But I don't think that was the intent. He didn't come to me with any hint of an accusatorial tone. He was sincerely questioning. And after I got past my standard, canned response about "seeking within" and started truly listening to his concerns and feelings, I began to really hear him. We practiced seeking within/among ourselves together, then in that moment.

After the workshop was over, this beautiful, graceful gentleman and I were walking together out by Ghost Ranch's labyrinth. "Well," he said. "I think what I appreciated most from this week was the community we built here together. The kingdom of God that we felt amongst ourselves here. I've got to thank you for helping us create that. But I still keep coming back to scripture. There's a scripture that says 'all of earth and heaven will one day pass away.' I take that to mean all we've talked about, all we've said about God and religion and so on, that it'll all pass away. Then the scripture says, 'but the Word of God shall last forever.' And that's what I've come to. The Word of God lasts forever."

"What's the 'Word of God'?" I asked, wondering if he were going to hold out his worn, black Bible that he carried in one hand.

An impish grin came across his face, then he leaned closer to me with an air of conspiracy toward what he was about to say. He said, "This right here, this love we've all been sharing. This community together. Close as I can describe it, anyway." Then he smiled widely and slightly lifted the Bible as well. "And this, too. It's the Word of God in here, too."

I listened and tried to keep an open mind. For this seeker, there were no contradictions between the love we'd all experienced together and the Word in his scripture. For him, the kingdom was amongst it all. And, it was his path he's traveling, not mine.

As we grow along our chosen spiritual path, we come to understand that each seeker must take responsibility for his or her own personal spirituality. Consider this: It is your experience of the Sacred and yours alone that you are embarked upon. If you consider yourself Christian, it is your personal awareness of the Christ or Holy Spirit *within you* that you seek. If you are Buddhist, it is Buddha nature *in you* you seek. This is true for all paths that I know of: Taoism, Native American Shamanism, Hinduism, Judaism,

Zen, and so on. It always returns to *your experience*. A Buddhist lama put it this way:

> There is a saying in Tibetan scriptures: "Knowledge must be burned, hammered, and beaten like pure gold. Then one can wear it as an ornament." So when you receive spiritual instruction from the hands of another, you do not take it uncritically, but you burn it, you hammer it, you beat it, until the bright, dignified color of gold appears. Then you craft it into an ornament, whatever design you like, and you put it on. Therefore, [the teaching of truth] is applicable to every age, to every person; it has a living quality. . . . The teachings are an individual personal experience, right down to the present holder of the doctrine.

You put it on. It becomes a living reality within and among your own life experience. The doctrinal teachings of your chosen spiritual tradition become an individual personal experience. Yours.

❧ 10

Honoring Life's Complexity

Oscar Wilde was referring to Honoring Life's Complexity when he quipped, "Only the shallow can know themselves." In truth, we human beings are emotionally and spiritually complex creatures, full of rich, deeply running waters.

MOST SEEKERS, MYSELF INCLUDED, FEEL A VERY STRONG attraction toward the ideal of an uncluttered, plain, and simple life. It's little wonder that books on "how to simplify" become bestsellers when our culture is overflowing with too much information, too much noise, and not enough times of quiet and reflection. And in many ways I'm a great advocate of simplifying life, of slowing down, hushing up, and contemplating the big questions that take lots of space and silence before we can even begin to approach them sincerely. Again, small wonder we are attracted to the idea of simplicity; we are so often starved for it. Starved.

And herein lies one of the great traps for any sincere seeker.

In our yearning for a more simple life, we may find ourselves attracted to a belief system—a theology or psychology—that offers the appearance of simplicity through clear-cut rules, laws, and easily-identifiable formulas of success by which to live. Such a "simple" belief system often promotes the illusion that, like the simplistic formula/model it advocates, the human condition is also easy to understand, or even master. The problem of course is that in reality neither life, nor ourselves, is ever that simple, nor understandable. It would be nice if life were, if we were, just *that simple*. But I've yet to meet a person who was "simple" emotionally, psychologically, or spiritually (we might even say morally or ethically, as well).

Of course we must seek tenets of spiritual truth and principles by which to live. And we need our spiritual codes of conduct. Still, we must also be wary of the all-too-human tendency to simplify and idealize our living principles into lifeless formulas that repress honest inquiry and questioning. A deeper spirituality asks us to acknowledge and even honor life's complexity. Oscar Wilde was referring to just this when he quipped, "Only the shallow can know themselves." The truth is, we human beings are emotionally and spiritually complex creatures, full of rich, deeply running waters. In our efforts to touch upon that almost Shaker-like sense of simplicity we so often crave, let's not seek the shallow pool of false mastery that arrogantly claims we fully know ourselves. Or someone else. Or God's wishes.

As the great teachers of our world's religions repeatedly remind us, much of life will remain clouded in mystery and unknowing. So while respecting the need to simplify in some areas of our life, you can also re-imagine spiritual maturity to include the cultivation, and even celebration, of life's complexity.

You may want to try this short mental exercise. I've found it a potent extension of Mr. Wilde's "only the shallow can know themselves" because it reminds me, experientially, that only the shallow can claim to wholly know *someone else*, as well. Here's the exercise:

Next time you think you have someone pretty much "figured out," consciously pause and try the following experiment. (This works especially well for those we live with: our spouses or lovers, children, parents, housemates, and so on; the closer we are to someone, the easier it is to think we *know them* completely.) Ask yourself if your "having figured them out" might be a form of reductionist thinking that makes *no allowance whatsoever* for other forces to be at work. Forces like the soul, God, destiny, or fate.

Notice if your assessment contains themes of over-simplification that claim generalized, clear-cut explanations like, "He's just jealous of my success, that's all," or "Instead of taking responsibility in an adult manner, she's simply blaming someone else for her own mistakes." Of course each of these examples could be a fairly accurate assessment of someone's particular action in a given circumstance, but the point is, they certainly don't provide "grand blueprints" to the entirety of someone's character, let alone soul. Most assuredly, our assessments are but *one smaller part* of a larger picture and movement.

Just take a moment and reconsider. Do you really have them wholly "figured out"?

❧

YES, WE CAN BE INQUISITIVE AND INTELLIGENT; WE CAN (AND must) seek to deepen our understanding of spirituality, psychology, and the way of living fully. Yes, we can work to heal addictive behavior and neurotic impulses; we can seek a spiritual system that helps us experience more peace and compassion in life—of course. Yes, it is our nature to seek. But what are we seeking? Some simple, complete, and finalized awareness to it all? Or peace? Do we want to have the Great Answer or inner peace, acceptance? I believe our knowledge and understanding of life is, ultimately, not only to help us live out our lives as human beings, but also to help us accept that there is so much more to "life" than we could ever control, change, or even begin to comprehend.

Finally, our exploration of spirit, psyche, and self reveals that this is an odyssey whose goal is not completion, but acceptance—acceptance of the Great Mystery that is always among and within us. An acceptance of life's complexity, and of our own complexity!

11

Remembering You'll Forget

You'll temporarily forget all those wonderful spiritual
and psychological insights you've learned—no doubt
about it. We all do. It's part of the great journey.

MY HOUSEMATE AND I WERE—OH, HOW TO SAY THIS IN
spiritually correct terms—working through our "relationship
issues," hip deep along the path of awakening via intensive
emotional processing. He'd just slammed the door to his
painting studio in my face. And I'd responded by yelling,
"Go to hell!"

My "Go to hell!" was somewhat disingenuous because I
knew all along that we had to go grocery shopping or we
wouldn't eat dinner that night. (And we had already missed
lunch due to our previous round of emotional processing
that morning.) So I knew I had him trapped when I yelled,
through the dark oak of his closed studio door. No matter
how intense, we simply had to go together to the grocery
store or we'd starve. It never occurred to me that he would
yell back, "Go to Albertsons—alone." We'd always gone to
the grocery store together.

By the time I'd finished shopping, I had chewed the

whole incident through a bit, but the bitterness still swirled in my mouth like burnt coffee. I loaded up the back of the Subaru with the formless plastic grocery bags and didn't faint, dammit. I slammed the hatch door shut with one hand and kept the cart from rolling down the asphalt incline with my other. For a moment I considered leaving the cart right there—my attack back upon the universe—but felt too guilty, too responsible, and so started the long push of the cart back to the sidewalk in front of the store where all good shoppers felt justified in leaving their carts.

Just as I passed the closest row of cars to the store, the handicapped row, an elderly white-haired gentleman wearing powder blue polyester pants gingerly shut his car trunk with one trembling hand, while holding his cart with the other. A cane was hung over the arm of his cart-holding hand.

Almost angrily I demanded, "Let me take that cart back for you."

He looked, slightly startled, frail hand still on the cart.

Then the world stopped as he smiled. Something broke. "Why, thank you, son," he said softly. "My goodness."

The Flow of Forgetting/Remembering

A deepening spirituality asks us to acknowledge and honor the space where we may temporarily forget all those wonderful spiritual and psychological insights we've learned along the way. If we don't give ourselves permission to be fully fearfully human at times, to *fully lose* our grounding, and *fully forget* the grace and perfection in life, we'll probably miss the moment of *remembrance*—when the world's spinning stops and something tight and closed within us blooms open.

I've told the story of the argument with my housemate and the resulting trip to the grocery store not only to confess to the reality of that particular relationship's own wonderful, fearful humanity, but also to demonstrate the flow of forgetting/remembering. This story witnesses the mysterious nature of our forgetting/remembering process. For example, forgetting can arise from the smallest, simplest of events. Often it is the little things in life that set us off on a spin (like the neighbor's dog defecating on the driveway, just under where my foot falls as I open the car door—this very morning's *major fit* of forgetting). Whereas just as often as not, life's big scenes bring with them an awareness of grace within the grit—a friend dying in the hospital, our heart opens to something larger amidst her pain—and forgetting is fleeting, if at all.

I've found that cultivating an environment within our minds that allows us permission to temporarily forget all our spiritual insights is necessary if we are, likewise, to allow ourselves to remember. It is also honest; because the reality is we forget and remember, forget and remember, again and again. If we are to honestly embrace the whole of our wonderful/fearful humanity, we must try to create an inner environment of mind where we honor our power as spiritual beings, while simultaneously honoring our everydayness, even our seeming powerlessness, as ordinary men and women living out our human lives.

❧

SOMETHING TO CONSIDER. NEXT TIME YOU "CATCH" YOURSELF coming off a bout of psychospiritual "forgetfulness" and you are beginning to remember the larger picture of life's journey, try to *feel* how the forgetting is intimately connected to your remembering now. Try to *feel* how the smallness and confining tunnel vision of forgetfulness (the texture of rage, prejudice, jealousy, and so forth) adds to the depth of your gratitude for this remembrance (of life's greater perfection and grace) now.

Do we really want the texture of smallness and spiritual forgetfulness to disappear from life altogether? Or does the contrast, this movement back and forth, serve a larger purpose?

Try to understand that, just as there are seasons of nature, there are also seasons of the heart. Sometimes we are in the closed heart of bleak, discontented winter. Sometimes it's the refreshing green liveliness of spring. Sometimes it's hurricane season.

Try to cultivate permission to ride the change and appreciate the diversity when possible—and to cultivate the quality of *remembering you'll forget* all those wonderful spiritual truths from time to time. Here it may prove helpful to repeat the advice that the Hindu saint Ramakrishna once gave to his students, "No matter how high the bird flies, it can always fly higher. There is no limit to realization, because Truth is an infinite sky."

❧

OUR WAY IS ALWAYS ONGOING, OUR AWAKENING AN INFINITE sky, an infinite depth. Forgetting, remembering. Fearful, wonderful. Remembering, forgetting. Wonderful, fearful . . .

12

Outrageousness

You can be eccentric, maverick, nonconformist, unorthodox, unconventional, distinct, and wonderfully, fearfully unique and free spirited—and still be authentically religious, authentically spiritual. The reality is, God works in not only mysterious but oftentimes outrageous ways.

CHRIS SITS ON THE FRONT PORCH OF MY APARTMENT IN Santa Fe. He looks out over the horizon toward the city below. "Sky sure is blue," he says, taking a drag off his cigarette. "A lot bluer here than in San Diego."

Chris is visiting me for the last time. At most, he has a few months left to live. Armed with a liquid morphine cocktail and Percocets, he is making his good-bye trip across the country. I'm the last of his friends he'll see before flying back east to visit his parents next week. Then he returns to his home in San Diego. Chris has one of those AIDS-related infections that no one had ever heard of ten years ago, but have become commonplace nowadays. He'd decided to stop taking all his medicines, except for the painkillers, and let himself die.

We sit silently for a few moments, both of us staring out

over the horizon. "You know," he says. "When those medicines were all out of my system I felt so much better. So
much. And it was *my* decision. I made it myself. I didn't
feel so helpless once I made that decision. But then I had a
new problem. What was I going to do with all this time
on my hands? I mean, I felt so much better, you see. I had
all this energy again, even if it was just temporary." He
throws his head back, laughing at the irony, then takes
another long drag off the cigarette.

Blowing a thin stream of smoke out between his lips,
Chris turns serious. "You see, I didn't want to wait around
to just die. I had to *do* something. Help someone, or something. You know, give something back. So I started working
with this volunteer program down at the AIDS center. I
began delivering flowers to people who were in the hospital.
I mean, I could still walk. I could go to the bathroom for
myself. And here are these people. In a room. With no
flowers. No friends. Only a TV set bolted to a bare wall.
Know what I mean?" Chris says. "They're dying fast. Most
of them have less than a week or two."

He becomes quiet for a moment. "Sometimes . . . Sometimes it's hard, you know. A lot of the people I take flowers
to have forgotten they're loved, you see. They've forgotten
and just think they're all alone. So it's hard." He pauses
again, then a mischievous, impish grin widens across his
face. "Well . . . I go into those rooms and show them
otherwise. You know, I bring them some flowers, fuss over

them a bit. And some of them are real hard, they just ignore you. Like you're not there." Chris barks a hoot. "Throw some of that attitude my way, girlfriend, and see what I can dish back."

He takes another drag off his cigarette.

"Know what I do? I just go over to the bedside. Sometimes I sit on the bed and sometimes I get right up in the bed with them—I mean, they can't give me that attitude crap, I've got AIDS, too—so I get right up in their faces and I just stare. I just stare at them deep, right into their eyes until they get it."

Again Chris becomes quiet, only glancing out over the horizon toward the far off Jemez Mountains.

"Until they get it?" I ask. "Get what?"

As he turns to answer me, I see a softness in his face that I'd not noticed before. For a moment his defenses are laid completely aside. "Until they get that I love them," he says gently, somewhat surprised. "Until they remember that there is such a thing as love, and they deserve it just like everyone else."

It is then I notice the tears welling up in Chris's eyes. "Sometimes you've got to fight hard to get someone to see that, you know. Fight real hard. But everyone I've gone to visit knows it. I don't leave until they look me back right in the eyes, until they know I'm loving them. That's what it's all about, you know. Loving them."

My friend smiles, blinking his moist eyelashes, then

brings the cigarette back up to his lips and takes a deep, deep inhalation.

"Yeah." Chris sighs. "That's what it's all about."

Chris was enrolled in the accelerated class of spiritual maturation that dying can sometimes offer. He began experiencing the value and importance of *outrageousness*. The tradition of outrageous wisdom has a long spiritual genealogy, spanning many different religious systems. Not only do we see it in Tibetan Buddhism in what one lama termed as "crazy wisdom," but it arises as the image of the wild Zen hermit, or as the God-intoxicated Hindu or Sufi master like Rumi, or as the "mad" monks of Christian mysticism. And so, too, in my friend Chris, in his climbing into the bed of a dying patient—outrageous wisdom inspired by love, by the sacred speaking within him. We see the quality of outrageousness at work whenever a seeker begins to fulfill his or her sacred individuality in a way that does not fit the prim and proper dictates of the day's current spiritual or social correctness.

Here, it is important to emphasize that being outrageous is not necessarily a loud and flashy endeavor. Authentic outrageousness has many different faces. If your soul calls for you to be subtle, soft, quiet, or demur in your expression of outrageousness, that is your way. The quality of outrageousness is not about degree, but about kind—a kind of authenticity that is true to your soul's innate individuality regardless of what other's say, regardless of the day's current climate of correctness. That's why it is viewed as outrageous. It shines a light from within yourself, manifesting the Sacred's glory, shining and giving others permission to do the same. Like my friend Chris, just before he died.

Thomas Jefferson's Outrageous Example

One of my favorite examples of spiritual outrageousness is found in the life of Thomas Jefferson. Just to scratch the surface of Jefferson's paradoxical and complicated life, we see the bright light of a renaissance man: keen intellect, philosopher, architect, designer, statesman, husband and father, amateur horticulturist and archeologist, writer, musician, Epicurean and wine connoisseur. And we can also see some darker shadows, a man whose brilliant idealism insisted that all people are created equal and endowed with inalienable rights from God, while throughout his lifetime he owned hundreds of other human beings. It seems that something powerful within Jefferson demanded that he speak these great truths, even if he were doomed to a degree of hypocrisy and failure when it came to trying to implement them into his actual daily life. But, regardless of how you feel about Jefferson as a slave owner, we must concede his brilliance as a thinker and statesman. He could definitely see the "bigger picture" that necessitated the eventual freedom of all people from slavery, as well as the separation of church from state.

To those of us who've studied his writings and life, it's no surprise that Thomas Jeffeson's powerful inner calling toward individualism deeply informed his spiritual life. Just as Jefferson spent years redesigning and rebuilding his tremendous home Monticello, he worked passionately on his personal rebuilding and reconstruction of Christian scripture. Like most of us who dare to ask the difficult questions, Jefferson struggled throughout his life to make sense of the teachings of Jesus as they appeared in the New Testament. And his ultimate solution was very true to his own spirit of individualism and architectural tinkering: audaciously cutting, rearranging, and pasting selections from the four gospels into one. Thomas Jefferson, the third president of the United States, edited his own personally relevant version of the gospels. In his way of seeing, he had extracted what he called the "gold" of authentic Christian teachings from the "dross," a corrupted text of the official church.

When I tell this story, I often see the shocked look of disbelief on a listener's face. *Heresy!* Or as one minister put it to me, "We don't have the luxury of choosing which scripture we like and which we don't. That's arrogance." Perhaps . . . and it is definitely outrageous. But it also is beneficial for us to remember that the text of both Testaments have undergone considerable revision and refinement in translation (and, to some degree, content) since the sixty-six separate books we now call the Bible were first compiled in A.D. 367. In the last century, especially, archeological discoveries of older and therefore more "original" Biblical texts have yielded significant changes in the way we read the Good Book. And I don't think any knowledgeable person could disagree with the fact that theological "higher criticism," which takes into account linguistic and other contexts from which the scripture arose, has revealed quite a different book from the King James Version our forefathers once swore by. (Since Jefferson's time was well before the higher criticism of Biblical scholarship, we might go as far as to understand his editing to be a personal attempt at early scholarship; Jefferson's text contained and juxtaposed the scripture in various translations, English, French, Latin, and the original Greek.) Regardless, the point is, Jefferson did not complete his final editing haphazardly nor without deep reflection. He knew the outrageousness of his action and chose to do it regardless.

Like it or not, Thomas Jefferson's individualized spiritual path included editing the gospels of the New Testament into a much shorter, less confusing text of his own—a personalized scripture that spoke intimately to his own mind and heart, and provided him with what he felt to be a more authentic vision of Christian life and teaching. In one of my lectures, I was once asked, "So, do you think Jefferson was a *better* Christian because of his audacity?" Well, depending upon your doctrinal and ideological take, you could argue either way. For me, personally, it's an irrelevant question, because *undoubtedly Jefferson considered this path a deepening of his own spiritual life.* The context in which I like to understand Jefferson's outrageousness is that he could not keep his soul's rich calling and enthusiasm toward intellect, individualism, and architectural tinkering separate from his religious life. He could not keep his soul's enthusiasms separate from his spiritual seeking. If we're honest about it, can any sincere seeker do otherwise?

❧

YOU CAN BE OUTRAGEOUS, WITH A WHISPER OR A SHOUT. What's important is that you are true to your own sacred individuality, to yourself. The reality is you can be eccentric, maverick, nonconformist, unorthodox, unconventional, distinct, and wonderfully, fearfully unique and free spirited—and still be authentically religious, authentically spiritual. Like my dying friend Chris, or Thomas Jefferson.

13

Grounding Yourself in the Extraordinary

A problem of seeking spirit in those big mystical experiences is that, in our single-minded pursuit of the spiritual "high," we often overlook the ordinary experiences that are before us in actual life—those extraordinary experiences of everyday life where the Sacred hides right here in plain view.

GOD IS ON THE MOUNTAINTOP, OR SO WE'RE TOLD. IT's a common image in most of our world's religions: the spiritual experience is imagined as a powerful moment of transcendence, above and beyond the ordinary, or worldly. So it's no surprise that we often associate the spiritual with those extraordinary, heightened moments of awareness, like standing on a high vista, overlooking the vastness of creation. Or sitting in a "blissful high" of prayer or meditation, absorbed by the awe of God within and around us. Both kinds of mystical highs—the mountaintop and the meditative—are legitimate aspects of the spiritual journey. Exotic and seemingly foreign to our modern, scientific view, these mystical experiences can introduce great inspiration into our lives, revealing a powerful vision of a larger "reality" that exists beyond the day-to-day awareness of our physical world. Often such experiences are profoundly transforming and healing; their power to shift our limited worldview is immense. But, as with all powerful experiences of light, there also exists a darker underside.

Misuse and misunderstanding of the mystical experience is a common pitfall for many seekers. It is quite tempting to feel yourself as being special for having had this type of experience. For example, the most powerful mystical experience of my life lasted for days, overtly affecting my behavior and perception for at least a month after. I became so certain that, *because of this*, I'd achieved a special spiritual status. After all, I'd experienced a "Big Event" I could point to and say "See, this was it." But, as the weeks passed, this specialness also passed in the light of everyday life. In day-to-day life, I found that I still had relationship problems, still became angry, jealous, even hateful at times. No matter how much I wanted to claim some finality to my spiritual awakening, the truth was otherwise. Though it was true that I had experienced *Something Inexplicable of God* in an intensity that I'd never before encountered, and it was true this experience did, in some manner, forever change me and how I see life, still . . .

Still, I had plenty of growing to left to do—and still do.

Perhaps the most enticing myth about the mystical experience is the misunderstanding that it will so utterly transform us that our lives will *wholly change* for the better. Part of the allure is that somehow this mystical, extraordinary window into God's Big Mind will be so shattering to our egoic little mind that—again, almost magically, instantaneously—we will be thrust years forward in spiritual development. It is tempting to think of the mystical experience as a change from without. "I don't have to do my daily grind of spiritual work because the mystical experience has thrust me past it all." But this is rarely, if ever, the case. Many seekers have been shocked to realize that after grand, even extended, periods of mystical experience (especially during intensive meditative retreats) they return home to find that the same old problems, patterns, and sufferings are still present in their marriage, family, and work life.

Also, it is quite easy to become attached to the "feeling" of the mystical experience. You can become a "spiritual high" junky, addicted to raptures, ecstasy, and visions. (Again, I speak from personal experience here.) Our mystical highs are no less addictive than the chemical high; and, if abused, they merely serve the same purpose—temporary escape from life's pain. I've already discussed how a mature spirituality seeks a kind of acknowledgment and acceptance of life's pain instead of avoidance and escape (—an acceptance in order to learn deeper lessons, soften and open our hearts, grow in soul and spirit). The problem with our attachment to the mystical and extraordinary experience is that, in our attachment or addiction, we will usually miss the very *extra*ordinary experience that is before us in every-day life.

A mature spirituality seeks to cultivate the awareness that Spirit is everywhere, not just at the heights of extraordinary, but also in the mundane, daily grind of the exceedingly ordinary. I like to refer to this quality as *grounding yourself in the extraordinary*. The pun helps me remember the larger cosmic joke. If we are to integrate our transcendent experiences of the mystical into the immanent experience of actual daily life, the quality of grounding ourselves in the extraordinary becomes an important practice to explore further.

There is no great secret here, just attentiveness and communion with those extraordinary workings of everyday human life. Psychologist Thomas Moore writes about how the daily chore of washing dishes after a meal becomes a spiritual practice, allowing him to connect with the depths of soul in ordinary housework, cooking, and cleaning. M. Scott Peck tells of how such mundane, daily routines as making one's 'to-do' schedule every morning can be a time of contemplation and connection with the divine. One Tibetan teacher would even go as far as to take his students on excursions to a nearby pasture, and while walking through the fields, find a fresh patty of cow manure over which he'd pause and instruct them to smell deeply, noticing the fertile pungency of aroma. "Notice how *rich*," he'd say with a smile, inhaling deeply.

*   *   *

When it comes to consciously cultivating the quality of *grounding yourself in the extraordinary*, the key is to keep your imagination alive and your mind open to the many daily possibilities. For example, a favorite practice of mine is to take a different route when going to the grocery store or on some other seemingly mundane errand. Even if it's a few blocks out of my way, I take in new sights—extraordinary sights of the city, the neighborhood—practicing being in the present moment, noticing the richness of experience around me, here, now: the trees, the neighborhood, the hitchhiker along the highway. That's how simple the quality of grounding yourself in the extraordinary can be expressed; in fact, that's the point. It's ordinary. This is a quality that reminds us our spirituality is not something to be practiced separate from our daily lives and routines; it's to be integrated, experienced within the whole.

Another favorite personal example involves email. For the last several years, I've tried to explore ways of keeping my imagination and connectedness to Spirit alive while engaged with my Macintosh. (Though it is currently in vogue to complain about the computer's impersonal nature, as a writer who's old enough to remember struggling with whiteout, I still bow in appreciation to my word processor's magic that makes wordsmithing a fluid process, rather than an painstakingly typed-out artifact.) As we become more and more technologically dependent, I believe we must begin to consciously integrate our computer and Web work into a spiritual practice of technology. Once, when overwhelmed by answering a batch of email just upon returning home from a long trip, the idea struck me to try a different approach to this magical form of communication. My different approach was to scroll down my personal on-line "address list" and, choosing one person at a time intuitively, send off a short email saying something like, "I'm thinking of you right now, a moment of prayer and gratitude for you in my life." I paused and consciously held each person in my mind for a few seconds before clicking the "send" button. It was a conscious prayer of blessing and gratitude that used the Internet's tremendous technology to connect me, in spirit, with dozens of friends. The whole affair took less than a half hour (and I've since done this with only one or two people, when they happen to cross my mind and my computer is on and email just a few clicks away). Why not? Also, such an email practice has the added gift of "arriving" to the person at some future time. When they read my prayer email, suddenly they connect back to me and the love that's within/among us both; what a tremendous way of personalizing a so-called impersonal technology. I've come to believe that such opportunities to creatively ground ourselves in the extraordinary are abundant and ever-present and are only limited by one's own lack of imagination.

Find your own everyday personal practices that remind

you of life's extraordinary richness and wonder. From washing the dishes and doing the daily household errands, to work-oriented tasks with the computer, our life is overflowing with opportunities to ground ourselves in the extraordinary of everyday spiritual deepening.

14

Talking Your Walk

The quality of "talking your walk" encourages you to look at your actual life experiences with openness, honesty, and awareness. We speak aloud and share the reality of our pilgrimage, grit as well as grace, so that we all may learn together.

DURING MY INTERNSHIP AT PARKLAND, I WAS ONE OF the few nonseminarians in the program. Most of the chaplains were ministers-in-training or already ordained and wishing to specialize in clinical pastoral care. It was quite an education for a lay person like myself. Daily I was faced with the challenge that an acute-care, urban hospital provides for any person of faith: to reconcile the distance between your *spiritual talk* on the one hand, and the real-life pain and suffering of your *actual walk* on the other. Most of us have heard the phrase, "walk the talk." It is an injunction for the seeker to try to live his or her life (that is, his or her walk) in accordance with spiritual beliefs (his or her talk). It's another way of saying that a sincere seeker tries to practice what she preaches, and this is always important if we are not to live a spiritual life of hypocrisy. But what was important for the chaplain staff at Parkland was for us to explore just those places along our walk where we were not able to live up to the talk. We were challenged to cultivate a larger faith wherein the doctrinal teachings of our spiritual talk could meet and be informed by the inner experience of our daily walk. There's perhaps few more potent places to do this than in the constant pain- and death-filled environment of a large urban hospital. Such an environment can make you question everything, every spiritual assumption and belief you've ever held. It is supposed to. That's the edge, where the deeper teaching of a life-integrated spirituality is to be discovered.

I witnessed my fellow chaplains, my patients, their care-givers and families encounter this edge on a daily basis. From middle-aged women dying of cancer to young men with AIDS, all kinds of faith, belief, and unquestioned doctrine were continually challenged, confronted, and put to the test of "real" life. Though more subtle, this lesson of integration is no less present in our mundane, everyday lives; we need not wait until the crisis of life-threatening illness to begin to seriously explore the edge of our doctrinal talk's relationship to our daily walk.

One way to begin this exploration is fairly straightforward: You discard the antiquated code of spiritually correct silence and begin to speak out. So often, in an idealized spirituality, we believe we must "walk our talk" no matter what. We believe we're not being truly spiritual if we admit to feeling "negative" emotions such as anger or rage. We're not truly spiritual if some horrendous event has brought us to doubt or question God's goodness. Often we believe to silently fake "walking our talk" even if to do so means we have to ignore our true feelings. The practice of *talking your walk* asks for just the opposite—to speak out. Instead of trying to fulfill the heroic model of Ideal Seeker, you can give yourself permission to be more honest about your actual real-life experiences. You muster the soft courage necessary to begin talking your walk aloud, with honesty and awareness, to sympathetic fellow seekers. This is one of the benefits of a good clinical pastoral education. Almost daily you meet with other chaplains and "talk" about your experiences—questioning, doubting, asking for advice, aid, and comfort, as you confront the disparity that sometimes exists between what you *want to believe* spiritually and what you're *actually feeling and experiencing* within your clinical work.

Unfortunately, most of us don't have the luxury of an institutional setting that encourages such honesty. More often than not, our religious institutions encourage us to tow the spiritually correct line without further exploration— that old-fashioned model of unquestioning faith. If you are blessed enough to be part of a spiritual community that encourages honesty and questioning, try consciously practicing the quality of *talking your walk;* let it become part of your communal as well as individual exploration. If, however, your spiritual community shuns such honesty, you'll want to cultivate your own cadre of seekers who will likewise commit to this practice with one another. The quality of *talking your walk* to another person allows you to excavate the grit of life that you might otherwise leave unacknowledged, giving you permission to hold the largeness of life's complexity, mystery, and uncertainty while still seeking.

Also, it is important to understand that the goal of *talking your walk* is not for you to, after talking, then fit your experience into a context of doctrinal correctness. The goal is *not* to find a spiritual trick of imagination that will magically soothe the pain that retelling your walk evoked; the goal is *not* to "fix" the walk. Rather, the aim is mainly to "talk" the walk and then let it be. Let it float—contradictions, complications, injustices, warts, and all. Let it float in the space within and among you. Yes, perhaps acknowledge how it hurts. Perhaps empathize (if you're listening to another talk their walk) because you've been there before and will probably be there again. Yes, you may offer care—empathy, consolation, or sharing of a way that you learned to "be present" within a similar situation. But, *and I can't emphasize this enough,* be acutely aware of any tendencies to obfuscate your walk's pain with those nice, clean, tidy bits of spiritual talk about "God's will" or the "universe's perfection" or whatever other platitude arises. Be aware of any attempts to avoid the uncertainties that you may experience in this practice.

Again, this is not to say that we can't offer each other spiritual advice; to the contrary. But do try to remember that the purpose of *talking your walk* is to expose and explore your real-life experiences within the context of a maturing spirituality; and that most often there will be no simple, easy answers to your questions. Again, life is much bigger than our theories of it usually allow. The quality of talking your walk purposefully cultivates the big questions when it comes to spirituality. It also cultivates a depth of permission and soft courage that bestows the sacred gift of honesty upon a fellow seeker, creating among you a community of spiritual sincerity, honesty, and depth.

That's a precious gift to give another person, and to yourself.

❧ 15

Embracing Opposites and Contradictions

Somewhere along the odyssey, one's spiritual sight begins to see beyond the narrow road of idealism and conceptual coherence. We look upon a wider landscape, from a view that's more accepting of life's inherent paradoxes and mysteries. And we become more comfortable with the contradictions and opposites we encounter along life's way.

DURING OUR LUNCH BREAK, DR. ROBERT CHESNUT, senior pastor of East Liberty Presbyterian Church in Pittsburgh, shared with our table a battle of conscience he was currently facing. A small group of old-guard church members plus a few young conservatives had attempted to oust his progressive ministry. Like many of the grand, august cathedrals of yesteryear, this one is now sitting in the urban heart of a bustling inner-city, whose residents run the gamut of race, ethnicity, and sexual orientation; and unlike many, this progressive church has grown with the times: it offers various kinds of worship services, from a weekly hand-clapping, gospel music celebration to the traditional Sunday sanctuary service; its activities range from Taize modern-day chanting to weekly labyrinth walking; the church provides an ongoing soup kitchen, food pantry, men's shelter, and tutoring program; all this, in addition to the full children and adult "spiritual life services and education" most have come to expect from a large Christian church. For some of the old-guard it was just too much—too much inclusion, too much liberalism, too much feminism, too socially activist, in short, far too progressive—and they wanted their "old church" back.

"How do you keep your heart open," the pastor sincerely asked, "when attacked and vilified? And from within your own congregation? I don't mean to tar everyone who disagrees with me with the same brush, but there was a hard core of bitter, mean-spirited, prejudiced people involved." He shook his head in disbelief. "And they're such a small, small group when compared to the entire congregation. Still, they've caused a lot of destruction to what we're trying to accomplish in our church." He paused and considered. "I'm trying my best to create a church of tolerance and inclusiveness. But, I'm faced with a paradox. If I practice what I'm preaching—tolerance—I'll have to show tolerance for their intolerance. And I just can't."

His battle of conscience: "The truth is, I have absolutely no tolerance whatsoever for their kind of intolerance. To bigotry and prejudice, I'm wholly intolerant. So, does this make me a hypocrite?"

Every one of us at the lunch table could relate to his dilemma. We've all been there in one way or another. As we discussed the pain that bigotry and prejudice caused in different aspects of our lives, we also began to seriously consider his question. "Maybe we can never be tolerant of intolerance," one person suggested. "If you're doing what's right, how can you be tolerant of someone's attempt to destroy your work?" asked another. Of course the example that came easiest to mind was how Jesus violently pushed over the tables of merchants in the temple (certainly an act of intolerance on his part), yet also taught to "turn the other cheek," an act of tolerance for sure.

"Well, I've come to only one conclusion with certainty," Dr. Chesnut said. We all waited. Then he smiled wryly with a wisdom that gets the cosmic joke of *embracing opposites and contradictions*, and continued, "An inclusive church is not for everyone."

As we spiritually deepen, we learn to be more comfortable with contradictions, seeming opposites and paradoxes coexisting side by side. We still question ourselves, and our path's contradictions and paradoxes, just like this pastor was doing at our lunch table that day. We still speak of our contradictions to others, we seek out advice and counsel. But, ultimately, there is wisdom in allowing ourselves to settle in, become more comfortable with our path's paradoxes, and embrace the wonderful, fearful reality of life's opposites and contradictions. If we don't learn to acknowledge and so *to see* the paradoxes that abound in life, we may miss many of the important lessons they have to teach us.

For example, almost a decade ago a friend once confessed his own internal conflicts regarding abortion. He said, in his heart, he believed abortion was the taking of life, perhaps even a form of murder. But his daughter had just begun her freshman year at college and was living out of the house, outside of his and his wife's watchful eye, for the first time. This troubled him considerably because he also knew that, if she came to him and with news that she was pregnant, he would not only encourage her to have an abortion so she could continue her education, but, as he said, "I'd even drive her to the clinic myself." This experience taught my friend that he had to soften his heart, make more room for uncertainties. It taught him tolerance. If he hadn't allowed himself to see the paradox, to admit it to—say, for example, since his daughter wasn't pregnant at the time, he could have just avoided thinking about the possibility altogether and stuck by his former opinions without considering the "what if"—he wouldn't have had to grow and soften his stance. He wouldn't have had to think outside of his doctrinal box.

The reality is that life is filled with contradictions, complexities, and difficulties that defy simple, black-and-white doctrine. We may be both for and against abortion; the death of a long-suffering beloved may be both welcomed and feared; we may crave the freedom to express our sacred individuality, yet cherish and need the community, ritual, and sometimes restrictive tradition of organized religion. Instead of "either/or," our journey is filled with "both/and."

We can also see the coexistence of contradictions and opposites in many of our great art forms. This is what the romantic poet John Keats was speaking of when, in a letter to his brother, he imagined what kind of depth and quality must be present in the person who creates truly great art or literature (in this case, Shakespeare). Keats believed that the true artist "is capable of being in uncertainties, mysteries, doubts, without any irritable reaching out after fact and reason." If there is indeed an art to living the sacred life, we might do well to listen to Keats's words and cultivate our tolerance of uncertainty, mystery, paradox, and contradiction within our own lives and spiritual pilgrimage.

In a manner, this entire book is about embracing seeming opposites, the light and dark, feminine and masculine, joyous and painful. Any person who has worked to recover from an addiction understands the necessary maturation of this kind of embrace—the alcoholic comes to understand that he must move beyond the early concretized "just say no" stance into the compassionate understanding of why he so wants to escape life through addiction. The same is true for the adult who was abused as a child: Though the abuse itself is inexcusable, compassion and understanding may eventually arise for the abuser, an understanding that they, too, were most likely abused as children themselves and are, perhaps, continuing the cycle of abuse as both victim and, now, victimizer. Again, "either/or" transforms into "both/and."

Somewhere along our odyssey, the spiritual path begins to expand from the narrow confines dictated by a rigid conceptual coherence, to the wider landscape of accepting life's inherent contradictions and mysteries. Here we may begin to recognize that life's ambiguities no longer trouble us quite as much as they once did or, as Keats would have it, life's mysteries are not quite as "irritable" as they once were. Contradiction and paradox are always right here in front of us. Embracing this reality is part of a deeper, maturing spiritual pilgrimage.

A well-known Zen story . . .

As student and Zen master walk together through a pine forest the student implores, "Please, master, speak to me of enlightenment."

The wise teacher points to a large, ancient pine. "Notice how tall that tree is?"

"Yes," answers the student.

Then the Zen master points to another tree. "Notice how short this other tree is?" he continues.

"Yes," the student replies again.

"There," says the master, "is enlightenment."

16

Discerning Love from Like

Fact is, the more spiritually mature a person becomes, the less they'll like some people—and that's why it's important to discern love from like. An authentic spirituality will not ask that we like everyone, but it will ask that we try to keep our hearts open, that we offer love to all people, even those we may rightfully dislike.

I USED TO BELIEVE THAT "LIVING THE SPIRITUAL LIFE" meant I should always focus upon the "good side" of a person. As my grandmother would say, there's always some good to be found in everyone. So I took her words, along with Jesus' admonition to "love your enemies," and the Buddhist principle of equanimity and nonviolence, and came up with my late baby-boomer, middle-class, white, American male version: A truly spiritual person likes everybody.

Well, it didn't take long to realize that trying to like everyone was not an easy spiritual ideal to uphold. For instance, I had one manipulative acquaintance who, given any opportunity whatsoever, would jump at the chance to spread ugly gossip and rumors about well-known personalities in the contemporary psychospiritual movement. Time and time again, I would go out of my way to keep an open mind about this person, insisting that I find the silver lining of goodness. Often I would hear how I—even after offering help—was the subject of his latest criticism and gossip. Why did I put up with this abusive behavior? The truth was, I really didn't like his behavior, really didn't like him. Still, I thought it my sacred obligation to try to like this person.

I went through a lot of personal torment—the equivalent of being a spiritual doormat—before finally recognizing my "like everyone" commandment for the gross over-simplification it was. In fact, my grandmother didn't say there is "only" good, but always "some" good. And I also see, in retrospect, that in regard to Jesus' words I'd confused "love" and "like." About the oft-quoted statement by Jesus, Martin Luther King, Jr. said:

And I'm happy that he didn't say, "Like your enemies," because there are some people that I find it pretty difficult to like. Liking is an affectionate emotion, and I can't like anybody who would bomb my home. I can't like anybody who would exploit me. I can't like anybody who would trample me over with injustices. I can't like them. . . . But Jesus reminds us that love is greater than liking. Love is understanding, creative, redemptive good will toward all men.

In my adherence to a spiritual correctness that said I must like everyone (and everyone must like me, but that's a whole other chapter), I had to turn a blind eye to much of the meanness that came my way. I'd confused love and like.

And . . . yes, I'm still working on it. For me it runs deep, an early-childhood river that flows through all of us who aimed to be "the best little boy (or girl) in the world." But Martin Luther King's view certainly gives me permission to be more honest about my feelings—and the permission to cultivate the quality of *discerning love from like*. I'm an openly gay man who, while writing this particular chapter, temporarily lives in a part of rural Virginia where ignorant acts of homophobia are as plentiful as pine trees. I can't truthfully keep in touch with my heart and also wish "my best" to the KKK—or, to a lesser extent, Jerry Falwell, who's less than an hour drive away.

But I can wish, can pray, that God's love enters their lives more fully, especially around all those unopened fearful boxes of prejudice and hatred they keep hidden within their own dark closets. I can keep my heart open and wish these people a deeper experience of the sacred in their lives, while also choosing not to personally keep their company, and to publicly confront their closed-mindedness. For me, this is a true challenge of spiritual depth: keeping my heart open, but giving myself permission to close certain social and relational doors—in other words, permission to not like someone, not keep their company, and, when appropriate, openly confront bigoted beliefs and mean-spirited behavior without hesitation. I can love Jerry Falwell as a wonderful, fearful human being trying to find his way closer to the Spirit, but I certainly don't have to *like* him. In fact, I can actively dislike him and the narrow-minded bigotry he represents.

Yet, the more important realization is that, if I'm allowed to recognize another's actions and not like him or her for them, I am also allowed to recognize similar prejudices *in myself* and not like myself for them either. If I cultivate this depth of permission, I can hear my soul's own innate wisdom, my conscience, whispering its truth, even as a conventional cultural, political, and spiritual correctness says otherwise.

❧

IMAGINE HOW SPACIOUS YOUR PATH COULD BE IF IT MADE room for the reality that you don't have to like everyone. That it is possible for you to keep your heart open, wishing another person a growing awareness of the Sacred in his life, while also choosing not to keep that person's company or condone his behavior?

That would be a much more inclusive path, one that doesn't turn a blind eye to the meanness that exists in our world—or in ourselves.

17

Personal Activism

To live the holy life is not only to think on God, but to work on ourselves. Not only to open our hearts in still silence, but to dance soulfully to a joyful noise. Sometimes we must sit upon a meditation cushion, sometimes we must take a stand. Either way, walking the sacred path calls for personal activism.

I HADN'T SEEN MY FRIEND SUSAN IN ALMOST TWO YEARS. After we caught each other up on recent events, she said, "Oh, I haven't told you, have I? I finally confronted my mother."

I must have looked puzzled because Susan started laughing, and I could tell she was laughing at me, at my expression.

"Not confronted confronted," she corrected. "We didn't all gather around and tell Mom she's got to go visit Betty Ford or else. Besides, she isn't drinking nearly as much nowadays." Susan laughed again. "What I mean is I spoke my truth, all of it. To her. And . . ."

Susan paused with a triumphant smile, then continued,

". . . Mom didn't *die!*" My friend nodded. "Despite decades of family mythology to the contrary, Mom didn't die!"

Now, to understand Susan's story, you have to understand a bit of the background of Susan's family. She was born to a well-to-do family in Dallas. All her life, she went to private schools and spent summers at the country club, was supposed to marry into her socio-economic class, preferably into another Texas family. And of course Susan did none of the above. Instead, she married a hippie type from Marin County, raised a child in California, became an alcoholic herself, divorced the husband when her daughter was off to college, sobered up, and—like so many of us in the midst of great life changes—moved to Santa Fe. Though she'd left "the Church" decades earlier, she was feeling a renewed interest in spirituality. In the last several years, she'd attended a retreat on the Christian mystic Hildegard von Bigen, participated in Native American sweat lodges, and meditated weekly at a Buddhist zendo. And now, at age 51, she was thinking about going back to school to get a certificate in massage therapy. In short, she was reclaiming her life, exploring her spirituality in ways that she'd never before considered, and doing "the work" as she called it, the work of psychospiritual exploration that was authentic to her soul's calling. And like many of us, she was a mess through much of it. That's how she and I became such good friends: We bonded through our honesty of seeking and our willingness to acknowledge our mutual messhood. Her confrontation with her mother had been the most recent exploration along her deepening way.

The confrontation was straightforward. Susan told her mother the truth of her life experience, as a child and as an adult. To simplify (for purposes of this story), her family mythology had always dictated that, above all else, you protect Mom. Protect Mom from Dad's abuse, his drinking, his sometimes violent outbursts, from his sexual acting out, from anything that didn't fit their perfect image of the ideal, country-club family. Susan and her two brothers both kept the secrets, or maintained "the lie," as she called it. In reality, of course, Mom knew all the secrets; she was, after all, present when most of the abuse happened. Still, no one was ever allowed to speak of this afterward, to do so might just push Mom "over the edge." (Susan's mother had cultivated that sense of fragility so well, her children took upon themselves the job to parent the parent.) After the death of Susan's father, twenty years ago now, the mythology hardened: No one was to speak ill of the dead, or of the family's pathological history. Despite the fact that both Susan's brothers had spent considerable time in and out of rehab over the years since Dad died, "it" was never to be discussed: not the dark secrets of their childhood, their father, their own problems with substance abuse, none of it. All was to remain a well-kept family secret; they had their good name and reputation to uphold. And, besides, everyone knew if they pushed too hard, Mom would simply die.

"After all the work I'd done, all the years of therapy," Susan said, "I still thought Mom would die if I mentioned any of it. Do my work with myself, with friends, and my therapist, but do not involve Mother. Mother was too fragile. Mother would shatter into a million pieces right in front of me and instantly die. Plus it would be my fault for bringing 'it' out into the light of day."

"So you confronted her," I added.

"Gently. I did it with compassion. I did it for me, *not* to punish her. I planned it carefully. I knew she'd be alone, without the housekeeper, on Sundays. So one Sunday afternoon, I sat her down and began. I told her, 'Mom, I've got to say some things. I've got to tell you about my childhood. I know you don't want to hear it and you think it's just bringing up old wounds from the past, needless pain. But I've got to tell you this for *me*. I need you to be brave and listen. I *need you* to do this for me, Mom.' So I started by telling her how much Dad's drinking scared us kids. How his anger terrified us and how some nights we'd all sleep together, huddled, hiding in the closet. Then, I waited to see."

"What'd she do?" I asked.

Susan smiled. "Nothing. Mom just sat frozen. Not a move. But most importantly, *she didn't die.* Then I thought to myself, 'Okay, look Susan, Mom didn't die. She's still sitting right here. You said one true thing and she didn't die.' So I told her something else. Then reminded myself to look at Mom, notice how she hadn't died yet." Susan laughed. "It really was like that. I'd pause and think, 'Okay, that didn't kill her. Let's try this one.' It took three hours. I've got to give her credit for that. She sat and listened to it all. I told her everything. How I felt abandoned, how at the time I hated him for years, how I felt guilty about drinking myself, about being drunk around my own kid. But I also told her how I'd worked through it, about my recovery. Telling her about *all of it* was one of the most difficult things I'd ever done. I tried to explain how I always thought she'd die if we spoke this aloud. I think she was kind of relieved, too." Susan's voice became so soft. "I really think she thought she'd die, too, if she ever had to hear these things."

My friend sighed. "So, we spent three hours, mostly me talking, but she did listen. And, at least twenty-five times, I consciously paused and thought, 'Okay, Susan. Look, she didn't die. You just said the truth here and Mom is still alive, sitting across from you.' "

The cool Santa Fe air blew between us and I whispered, "Wow." Susan nodded. "Yep," she returned, "big wow."

I grinned. "So, she's still alive, right?"

Susan laughed. "And kicking. It really was tremendous for me. I just had to tell her the truth. Finally. It was one of the most important things I've ever done in my life."

"And now—?" I said, pausing.

"Well, now, of course . . ." Susan smiled then shrugged. "Now, we have the fact that Mom didn't die when confronted with the truth."

"But are you closer?" I asked. "I mean, now. After this talk?"

"Well, I am. I don't think it really changed a thing for Mom. She's still back in her little dream world. But I *know* the truth didn't kill her. And I now know that the truth won't kill me. Or anyone else. That was big for me. All my life I'd believed the truth could kill. Would kill. I can't change Mom. But I'm working hard to change the way I relate to her. And to everyone else." She became quiet for a few moments. "Especially with myself. Everyday I remind myself that the truth does not kill you. It can be spoken."

We settled into a kind of sacred silence, both honoring the soft courage of her honesty. Both honoring the story she'd told. Both remembering why we loved each other.

I believe every seeker will, at some point along the way, become an activist for his or her personal truth, for honesty of heart. The leap into this quality of *personal activism* is something we undertake in order to remain true to our innermost self. It's a quality we come to cultivate, again and again, as we encounter new obstacles and opportunities along life's pilgrimage. We've got to speak out for ourselves, for the sacred nature of life. And make no mistake about it: Endeavoring to be true to your sacred individuality and to honor that individuality in others *is* an activist stance in our culture.

Another example, from my own personal odyssey:

Several years ago, before the powerful new HIV drugs appeared upon the medical scene, I remember a point in my life when I was working on inwardly acknowledging and accepting my own dying process, including my "full blown" AIDS diagnosis. I'd started receiving Social Security Disability only a few months before and was encountering feelings of personal failure and shame. One of the practices of honesty I began during this time was to be truthful about my "job." I like to write at coffeehouses, and often someone would say something like, "You know, I see you here all the time. What do you do for a living?" Until that point, I'd always responded that I wrote and lectured on spirituality and its relationship with life-threatening illness. Though I was still writing and occasionally lecturing, in order to honestly integrate and accept my health's decline, my own physical dying process, I knew I had to be more up-front about how I managed to pay the rent and bills. (Because certainly my writing and lecturing were no longer bringing in enough money to cover living expenses.) So when someone would ask me what I did for a living, I'd answer, "I have AIDS and I'm disabled." For me, that honesty was a kind of personal activism, where I told the truth, refused to hide my reality and to begin to work consciously with my own dying process. At the time, I called my practice "living my dying."

At the time . . .

How a seeker's personal activism manifests itself often changes over time, as you mature, as life's circumstances change. My friend Susan had come to the point where her own personal activism of spirit demanded that she break, for herself, the myth that others would die if she spoke the truth. It was an intense personal activism.

Many of us can relate in our own way. How often does someone ask, "How are you?" Often our response is, "Oh, fine," when, in truth, we're not fine at all. Yes, culturally, this kind of greeting is not usually intended to be sincere; we're *not* supposed to actually go into a detailed account of our lives: "Oh, I'm not doing so well today; the neighbor's cat just got run over by a car, my brother-in-law has cancer, and I think I might have a kidney stone." No, we've cultivated a society of disinterest, dishonesty, and disingenuous care. "Oh, fine. I'm fine . . ." The quality of personal activism pushes you to demonstrate against this kind of dishonesty. Next time you're asked, "How are you," you could answer truthfully, yet tactfully. Something like: "I'm not so well today, but I'll get by. I really don't want to go into detail if that's all right with you." Or, if you are "fine," do say so. But try not to lie just because it's easier, or expected. The problem with this kind of activism is that, like the animal rights activist who throws fake blood on the unsuspecting person in a fur coat, we are likely to get exiled for our actions. One seeker, who was trying a practice of honesty to the "How are you doing?" question, reported that because of her honesty she was ridiculed by her fellow co-workers throughout the day. Either someone would make it their duty to try to cheer her up—to cure her, not care for her—or she would be passively shamed. "Better take it easy with Ellen over there, she's feeling sad today," a co-worker would say in a mocking voice, purposefully loud enough for her to overhear. Let's face it, we are not a culture that accepts emotional honesty with grace and ease. It takes a personal activism to be true to yourself in today's society.

I remember once hearing an interview with Maya Angelou. The poet said that, if someone who is a guest in her house says something she considers to be vulgar or mean-spirited, she confronts them about it immediately. She tells them in no uncertain terms to "Stop!" or leave; this choice is up to the guest, but it is Angelou's house, her living space (I like to imagine "living space" in a larger, figurative sense) and she will not have anyone desecrating this space with mean-spirited or prejudicial remarks. I've often imagined what it would be like to have Dr. Angelou's forceful presence in my face, giving me such an ultimatum. I've often wondered why I didn't find the courage to say, "Stop! Or leave!" to someone who was in my "living space" when they displayed mean-spirited bigotry of some nature. So often, we just politely smile and turn away from such pain and awkwardness. We think, why compound the painfulness of the situation by confronting someone, here, in my space? Why not just let it pass on by, unencumbered? And sometimes, letting an offense pass us by may be the correct thing to do. But other times, perhaps if we were in touch with the quality of personal activism, we'd recognize that now *is* the time to speak up, to say "Stop!" To another, or to ourselves. Stop lying about your AIDS diagnosis, Joseph. Stop dancing around the myth that the truth will kill your mother and everyone else as well, Susan. Stop . . .

❧

CONSIDER THIS: AT EVERY POINT ALONG ONE'S JOURNEY, there are important issues and insights to be explored: cruxes in life that call for a quality of *personal activism*. Sometimes these involve declarations of self-honesty, other times a kind of self-vigilance (such as catching yourself exaggerating a story, or perhaps passing on hurtful gossip). These discoveries, in all their varied forms, are potent opportunities for personal activism.

There is a popular misconception many people have about activism: that it must be dramatic and somewhat anger-filled. In this misunderstanding, activism is viewed primarily as an outer posture, an external event. But a personal activism begins within, an inner call of recognition for your life to actively reflect and demonstrate the truth of who you are, the truth of your sacred individuality. No one else can authoritatively tell you how your activism should manifest itself. Such an activism is, finally, between you and your heart, between you and your God. And, as I said, I believe we, throughout our entire lives, are always presented with opportunities for this kind of deepening and personal activism.

What is your opportunity for personal activism today? At this place along your journey, right here—what's the area of personal activism that is calling out for your attention?

And are you willing to act?

18

Allowing Forgiveness to Take Its Time

If we rush forgiveness, we'll most likely miss the lesson we're being asked to learn. And we'll probably not truly forgive, either.

MY FRIEND CATHERINE AND I WERE HAVING THE USUAL Monday breakfast at our favorite coffee shop, when the talk turned to the movie *Dead Man Walking*, and how it plucked away at our heartstrings. The movie is a depiction of the true story of a Catholic nun, Sister Helen Prejean, and her experiences as spiritual advisor to a convicted killer during the final weeks leading up to his execution in prison. Our discussion turned to a scene near the end of the film, after the murderer had been executed. Sister Prejean is standing alongside his freshly dug grave as the short funeral service concludes. As she turns to leave, Prejean notices the father of one of the victims observing from a distance. Like her, this man is a devout, practicing Catholic. Evoking further the painful and confusing process they've both just undergone—him as the grieving father of the victim, her as the advisor to the murderer—he says to her, "Sister, I don't know why I'm here. I've got a lot of hate. I don't have your faith."

"Faith?" Prejean replies. "I wish it were that easy. It's work." After an awkward moment, she continues. "Maybe we could help each other find a way out of the hate."

His response cuts to the bone. "I don't know." Then a quick breath, "I don't think so. I should go."

My friend Catherine shook her head. "Can you believe it?"

I remembered the scene as Catherine continued, "He was so honest. So brave. He was saying, 'I need this anger. I cannot let go of it yet. For me to forgive so quickly and easily would be untrue to the deep pain I feel about my son's murder. Untrue to my grief right now.'"

My friend's eyes narrowed. "And then the most amazing thing happened. I realized that this is exactly how I feel about my ex-husband. It would be dishonest for me to forgive him right now. To 'let go' of what happened, right now, would not respect the reality of this process I'm still going through. It would be a lie."

I didn't respond at first and Catherine grinned during the long pause that followed. She knew she was bordering on spiritual heresy.

Perhaps there is no part of the psychospiritual path more idealized and moralized than forgiveness. In eastern spiritual traditions it is considered one of the best ways to burn karma. In many pop psychology and New Age circles it is the magic key to releasing all one's problems and ailments. And in Christianity, citing Jesus himself who forgave those who were crucifying him because "they know not what they do," forgiveness is envisioned as an ultimate act of human redemption. It is that most-hallowed, universal, and unquestioned injunction of spirituality—thou must forgive, or else. And, it is a huge problem for most of us.

Now, the problem with forgiveness is certainly not the healing and releasing attributes that authentic forgiveness elicits (that's the grace, the reason we're doing the "work" of forgiveness in the first place). The problem with forgiveness is when it becomes an unexamined, formulaic application; when it is viewed as a one-time-get-it-over-and-done-with *event*, rather than a *movement* within an ongoing, larger process. How often have you gone to great lengths to try to forgive someone, only to find that—though you thought you'd done it, thought you'd finally forgiven them, were "over it" and had continued on with your life, clean slate in hand—only to find that, in an instantaneous eruption, you were still mad as hell. It may have taken a grocery clerk mumbling under her breath at you, or a teenager in his jacked-up pickup cutting sharply in front of your little Honda sedan, but, whatever, you were still mad as hell all over again about that same old thing. Your forgiveness failed; your anger still present as ever.

Usually the subtext to our spiritual correctness seems to be that we should forgive immediately—"let go and let

God," as the popular saying goes. And if we don't, if we hold on to our unforgiveness, we may be spiritually shamed for it. Although a willingness to forgive is indeed a good place to start, the spiritually correct assumption is that the better seeker would instantly forgive and move on. Here, it is important to remember that spiritual correctness is not necessarily spiritual maturity. Perhaps we might reconsider such a simplistic view of forgiveness and, instead, honor life's complexity within our "work"—as Prejean put it—of ongoing faith. A maturing spirituality asks us to question how a rush into forgiveness might *not* be the authentic sacred or soulful way for an individual seeker in a particular circumstance. This is what my friend Catherine was talking about that morning over coffee.

Long moments of silence passed between Catherine and me as my mind wrestled with what she had said. I hadn't yet come to the point where I was willing to question my rush to forgiveness in this circumstance. When I saw that scene in the movie, my mind had retreated into a subtle form of either/or fundamentalism, interpreting the father's lack of forgiveness as a kind of "human" weakness that was purposefully juxtaposed to Sister Prejean's larger "spiritual" magnanimity. I'd understood the scene in a wholly different way, a directly opposite interpretation to that of my friend. But I trusted her instincts here. My relationship with Catherine had long since demonstrated that we both had a lot to learn from one another.

I continued cautiously. "So, do you want to forgive your ex-husband?"

"Yes, yes. Absolutely, I do. Of course I want to forgive him and I'm sure I will. I mean, I brought the question up—'Can I forgive him?'—because within me a higher knowledge knows I'm going to have to anyway. But the honest answer to my question *for now* is, 'No, I can't forgive him yet.'"

She reached over, gave me a reassuring squeeze of the hand, and smiled. "And, yes, I'm very clear that the reason I want to forgive him is because I don't like the hatred *in me*, the feeling of anger *I'm* stuck with right now. I don't want to forgive him to take care of him . . . I want to forgive him to take care of me. And that scene in the film gave me permission to do that. To let my forgiveness take the time it needs. I'm not a spiritual retard because I can't forgive him right away. I'm actually honoring the reality of my process."

Taking Time

How often in our goal of spiritual propriety do we try to gloss over the time and space necessary for healing? This is not to say that time itself is the healer; in my experience, time itself does not heal. Rather, time is the container in which forgiveness and healing works its alchemy. And if we attempt to rush the process too much we may end up with a bastardized mixture of metal that is neither lead nor gold. In a simplified spiritual correctness that emphasizes a rush to forgiveness, we try to separate the grace-filled *event* of forgiving from the messy, sometimes lengthy *process* beforehand. The reality is that authentic forgiveness does not often exist in a vacuum; usually it is worked for over time. Working through this process is usually painful, filled with anger at the injustice done, at the perpetrator, at life, sometimes at God. The process beforehand involves putting the accused "on trial" so to speak, and honestly so. In any situation there are many lessons to be learned, but we must go through the trial to see these lessons clearly. If we try to magically jump into the posture of faux forgiveness, we miss the lessons that arise beforehand. Though instinctively the spiritually-maturing seeker, like my friend Catherine, recognizes that, yes, she must eventually arrive at forgiveness—for her own sake and peace of heart—she also understands the larger responsibility to honoring the sometimes slow and painful journey of getting there. Inevitably, within this journey, a sense of morality and ethics begins to deepen, an awareness of responsibility to and for actions taken. There are many potent lessons within the process of working toward authentic forgiveness. You don't want to miss them. As the saying goes, it's not just the destination, but the journey, too.

Authentic forgiveness acknowledges the reality of your life's process. It allows you time, honoring your anger, your need to hold on to that anger for a time, to chew it through and digest it thoroughly. It allows you to learn from your circumstances, to recognize a wrong and label someone's actions as such. Authentic forgiveness encourages faith in the greater life-lesson at work, the larger movement of humanity. That is what my friend was speaking to that morning over coffee, a larger vision of faith. She had rediscovered a larger faith in her soul's growth process.

"I would really like to let go of my anger," Catherine said again. "But I also know I must honor all these feelings I'm still having. I'm coming to forgiveness, real forgiveness. I know it. But it's going to take as long as it needs to. If I rush it, it'll be phony and partial. Within myself, I know I'm just not ready to fully forgive my ex-husband yet, and that's okay for now. It wasn't before. But it is now."

Catherine sighed, then she laughed. "Well, I guess I'm not a spiritual retard after all."

❧

ARE THERE ANY ISSUES OF FORGIVENESS THAT YOU'VE TRIED TO rush because it was the spiritually correct thing to do? Can you allow yourself permission to re-open those closed boxes and let in some fresh air and light? Perhaps discuss this issue with a compassionate friend. A friend who understands that you need to take the time to authentically heal. A friend who knows not to put the box's lid back on so quickly. Not just yet. Perhaps pray together for your forgiveness to deepen. Talk the reality of your walk, letting the honesty of fresh air and openness work its alchemy upon your wounds. And honor your soft courage for doing the difficult work of authentic spiritual maturation and forgiveness.

19

It's Never Too Late

Teachers arrive in all kinds of costumes, in a myriad of situations. They step into the role of friends, family, and strangers, giving us chance after chance to grow and heal. Though we may continue to avoid an opportunity to deepen spiritually, it's never too late. Always our teachers return, in yet another guise. Again and again until we learn.

THE DOCTORS GAVE MY OLD FRIEND ANN ONE MORE day to live, two at the most. A week later she still hung on, comatose, lips cracked and bloodied from labored, dry breaths. I'd avoided going to see her. The truth: I just couldn't take it. Not another person's deathbed. Not now. Not Ann. Secretly I'd hoped she'd die as the doctors predicted, quickly and quietly.

After a week of avoidance, I finally gave in and went to see her out of guilt. Guilt that I'd not gone earlier, and guilt of a past we both shared with an abusive spiritual teacher. Years ago, I'd introduced Ann to this teacher who was so quick to tell those of us who were diagnosed with any kind of life-threatening illness that, "In God's reality there is no death; death is merely a human illusion; you need only see past this illusion and death will vanish." At the time, I was so eager to escape the constant death and dying around (and within) me, I'd run headlong toward this simplistic teaching of eternal life with all my might. Understand, this self-proclaimed "enlightened teacher" was not merely espousing that an eternal soul-nature continues to live after the body dies. To the contrary, he was teaching that if we simply "perceive" the body and its problems of aging, illness, and death as "illusions," we can re-vision our body as "perfect," and so achieve a kind of physical immortality. "If you realize the perfection of God within you, the illusion of death cannot conquer you," the teacher would proclaim. He cited Jesus' resurrection as evidence.

Unlike myself, Ann had been slow to embrace this man's literalist take on spiritual healing. But after several years, as her cancer treatments failed, she began to consider more desperate options. Maybe what this unusual teacher had to say was true, maybe we could escape illness by "surrendering" ourselves totally to God's law—and, of course, surrendering ourselves beforehand to the teacher as a sign of good faith. (Sound familiar?)

I'd long since left the teacher and his cultish community by the time Ann became so desperate that she was willing to give this abusive man's message a closer look. But when Ann, barely 100 pounds and losing hair from another failed chemotherapy effort, arrived at the community, the teacher pointed a menacing finger at her and snarled, "You come here with your illusions of sickness and death. I won't have it. Get her out of my sight!" Oddly, Ann didn't blame him for this flagrantly mean-spirited and uncaring abuse. Such was Ann's state of confusion that she took the attack to heart. "I've fallen into the illusion of dying," she told a mutual friend. "If I could only see the perfection of God, this illness would vanish."

I was furious when I heard about what the so-called enlightened teacher had said to Ann, and even more furious with Ann's tepid response. At first it angered me that Ann would agree her illness was witness to a spiritual "failure" on her part, then I felt guilty. I felt guilty because I'd told Ann and many others just that same line—"Illness is an illusion!"—so many times before. And I couldn't escape that I was, at least to some degree, responsible since I'd introduced her to this insulting and cruel teacher in the first place. This was why I avoided going to see Ann as she lay dying in the hospital. I avoided her for that entire week, but she wouldn't die. I can see now how it took that much time for me to recognize that I couldn't escape after all. There was something I needed to ask.

Ann was comatose when I arrived at Baylor Hospital. Her mother and sister took the occasion of my visit to go to the cafeteria and take a break from the deathwatch. Only one other person was with us in the room—Rick, one of Ann's oldest and best friends. He gave me a hug. I'd introduced Rick to the teacher at the same time I'd introduced Ann.

I stood by Ann's bed and began caressing her face, brushing her thinning hair—once so beautiful, blonde, and thick—back off her forehead. She had absolutely no physical reaction to my touch or to any of my words. When I next looked up, two other people had joined us in the room. Carlos and Dana—both of whom had spent time at the abusive teacher's community as well. A coincidence?

Within minutes the room was filled with six visitors including me—each of us having been to visit that same teacher at least once, each having once embraced the literalist "there is no death" doctrine to some degree before coming to see how our spiritual literalism had gone astray.

I put my palm flat on the crown of Ann's head, reaching my other hand out to Dana. She joined me, as did the others, and we formed a healing circle around the hospital bed. Carlos stood on the opposite side of the bed and took Ann's hand to complete the circle.

We closed our eyes together and I led us in a prayer. Before saying "Amen," I paused. It was the time and place to end the prayer, to be officious, but I couldn't. I had to finish something larger.

"Ann," I whispered. "If you can hear me, I need your forgiveness. I was wrong about death being the opposite of healing. Death can be a healing, too. I was so wrong. Your dying now is *not* an illusion, or failure. It's part of your greater healing. I was completely wrong." My voice began to crack. "Please forgive me, Ann."

No other sounds except for the labored breathing. Of course Ann didn't respond verbally in any way to my request. The steady, labored breathing merely continued. I looked into her face, her closed eyes and dried lips, and reminded myself about the studies done with coma patients and their ability to hear and sense what's going on around them.

Then from within the silence of the room, I heard a small voice coming from the foot of the bed. It was Rick. "Joseph, I forgive you," he said softly.

I felt Dana squeeze my hand, and she, too, said, "Joseph, I forgive you."

Then, "Joseph, I forgive you," Carlos also said. "Joseph, I forgive you," said another. "Joseph, I forgive you," came again from another.

Then Rick said, "Dana, I forgive you." And the circle obliged, everyone taking turn saying, "Dana, I forgive you."

Then someone said, "Rick, I forgive you." And again the circle obliged, everyone forgiving Rick.

This continued, one by one, through the circle around Ann's deathbed until we reached Carlos and everyone forgave him as well. For a moment we were all still, silent.

I took a deep breath and said it. "Ann, I forgive you."

Then from across the bed, Carlos said, "Ann, I forgive you."

In a whispered rush, everyone around the circle began to say, "Ann I forgive you." We whispered this over and over, a gentle continuous canticle to our dying friend. "Ann, I forgive you. Ann, I forgive you."

Beneath our soft words we became aware of a faint sound. A strange noise rose up into the room before us, floating on its own, a background pitch to our chant of forgiveness.

Through Ann's lips a long slow moan of release let out with her breath. There was a pause as Ann inhaled. Then the slight moan rose into the room again.

We stared at our friend's motionless body. She was making a sound. Ann heard us and was responding.

This was Ann's last sound. She died later that night.

No, it's never too late.

20

Inviting Fear to Tea

A deep spirituality will not ultimately save us from the pain and confusion that is often present in our lives. But it can help us be fully present and awake to the great lessons and larger joy of our wonderful, fearful creation. It can help us invite our fears into a kind of intimacy so we might come to know and love ourselves better, warts and all.

DESPITE ALL THE INTENSIVE PERSONAL AND PROFESsional work I've done with loved ones and patients who were dying, still, whenever I first visit someone who is nearing the final days or weeks of the dying process, I experience it. "It" is what I characterize as a "little fear" that pulls and tingles deep insight my gut, just below the navel. The visual image I hold of this little fear is like a peach pit: that hard, shriveled, but hollow core at the center of a peach. It is a tightness that, if I let it continue unnoticed and unacknowledged, will expand to grip my entire mind and body. In my first book, I confessed that this hollow core is the secret, personal place where I do some of my most earnest work of letting go and opening. That remains true to this day.

One of the insights I've gained from this ongoing experience is to recognize that this fear, if acknowledged and accepted into my emotional reality, can become something *other* than the fear itself. If I'm conscious enough to begin to open to my fearful experiences, often these experiences begin transforming from the hard, tight pit of retraction into something else entirely—something gentle and soft, a whisper that calls me deeper toward grace.

But, still . . . It certainly wasn't always like that, and this metamorphosis didn't just begin to happen overnight. Those I know who have experienced this deepening and transformative process with their fears all agree: It takes time and effort on our part; it takes dedicated work on letting go *into* the fear. So how does this happen? How do we encourage this process of graceful transformation?

The best mythological image I've found for embracing our fears is not Western in origin. It is a story about the great Tibetan saint, Milarepa, who lived over 800 years ago. In the myth, three demons come to haunt the venerable saint as he meditates alone in a cave. We can understand these creatures to be the inner demons and conflicts—the many fearful emotions, great and small—that arise in daily life. According to legend, as the demons enter into the calm meditative space of his cave (his conscious experience), Milarepa smiles and welcomes them, urging them to sit with him by the warm fire and to "take tea." The demons bark,

"Aren't you horrified by our arrival?" And Milarepa responds, "Oh, not at all. It is at moments such as these that I am reminded to have compassion and mercy for myself. When the demons of fear, doubt, loathing, and anger appear, I am most grateful to be on the path of conscious spiritual growth, for then I can welcome you and open my heart to you, instead of running away and hiding. So, please, come and sit. Take tea with me. You are always welcome to emerge from the darkness and sit with me by the light of the fire. For it is only here that we may take tea together."

The point of the story is that, not only does Milarepa acknowledge the inner demons as they arise, he goes even further by *inviting them into intimate relationship*, to take tea with him by the fire's warmth and light. Continuing the metaphor, we might see the light of the fire as representing the illumination that sometimes comes from fiery circumstances in our lives. Instead of pushing our fears away, we can invite them to join us beside the fire of consciousness itself. Though we may be in some manner "turning up the heat," we are also increasing the potential for illumination. Likewise, if we invite our fears to join us in a deeper intimacy—to take tea with us—we can begin to understand that our fears are also *living creations* within ourselves. Perhaps we may begin to honestly and compassionately say, "You're not so frightful after all. You just need to be acknowledged and honored for being part of me. In fact, I bet you have a lot to teach me about myself. Share your inner heart and wisdom with me, my fear, as we sit here together and share this tea."

A few years ago I have no doubt that I would have been ashamed of my "little fear" that arises when first entering the room of someone who is dying. The voice of spiritual correctness says, "Shouldn't someone as experienced and 'spiritual' as you be beyond this, Joseph?" And make no mistake, that voice still speaks inside my head. It's not that all my years of psychospiritual work have silenced the voices of doubt and fear. The difference is that now I try to invite them closer to the fire, to sit and have tea so I can hear what this part of myself is truly saying—like, perhaps, "I'm still scared that we're not good enough, Joseph; what if we try faking it so others will think we're good enough, then maybe we can believe it ourselves?" When I'm aware of this dialogue and when I honor it, I can have tremendous compassion for these demons, these parts of myself.

So, today, I *try* to invite the fearful demons within me— anger, rage, jealousy, boredom, prejudice, and so on—to tea so I might cherish an intimacy with them. Everyone finds his or her own ways of inviting fear to tea. Talking your walk with an understanding and compassionate friend (a kind of confession, really) has been, for me, a good way to start. But there are many ways to explore this legitimate and, I think, necessary part of our spirituality. For most, any form of self-exploration that involves the creative process is a good tool for this kind of self honesty. In my workshops, after describing Milarepa's story, I've asked participants to do brief timed writing exercises where they imagine themselves to be sitting in the cave and one particular demon comes calling. In their writing exercise, they are to name the demon, write of its characteristics, and then, most importantly, to invite it to speak to them. They then write out what message and/or wisdom the demon has to teach them about themselves. But, each seeker needs to find their own individualized ways and techniques of inviting their fears closer. I'm a writer; it's no surprise that a writing exercise would be one of my preferred methods—but, and this is crucial, it may not be your preferred way. Explore other expressive forms, perhaps guided meditations or dream analysis. And don't forget to honor your own sacred individuality along the way. We are all wonderfully, fearfully made. Our fearful inner demons serve as reminders that we're human, after all, and that we still have more lessons to learn, deeper to go, and more heart to open.

❧

SPIRITUALITY WILL NOT SAVE US FROM THE NATURAL PAIN AND confusion of our human journey. Instead, spiritual awareness offers us encouragement to be fully alive and present to the situation of life as it is. Though a pop-spirituality may provide "The Big Spiritual Answer" as a defense against life's uncertainties, a mature spirituality opens into that very same unknown, into the whole mysterious process of human life itself. It is here, opening to heart and to our own wonderful, fearful reality, that we begin to approach our fears differently, with an intimacy, a soft courage, and a willingness to practice *inviting fear to tea*. It's a delicate image, yourself and fear, sitting together over tea. Delicate and to be cherished.

21

Letting Be, First

We've all wanted to magically give our problems—often our learning opportunities—away to the caretaker God. "God," many a seeker has said, "I give this to you." But sometimes what we actually mean is "Here you go, Spirit, I don't want to learn from this. Just get rid of it for me. Thanks."

OFTEN I HEAR SOMEONE WHO'S REFERRING TO A PROBlem say, "I just let go of it." But, again, what is sometimes meant by this is, "I'll just close my mind to this problem so it will hopefully go away." My experience is that before we can "let go," we've got to be able to just "let be." If we are not content to first just let things be, we are usually still attached to the problem being magically and instantaneously gone. And attachment is *not* the essence of letting go. If we let be—just be here, right now—we'll find out if we have any hidden grasping attachments, secret stashes of avoidance where we don't care to learn from life's circumstances, only to escape them.

Consider, when you say "let go," what are you really saying? Let go of what?

I like to imagine that what we are really letting go of is

the lie. The lie that says, if we "hold on" tight enough, life can be controlled. The lie that says, we can prevent change (which is often painful) from happening to us. The lie that says we can successfully hold or even stop life's flow; that we can defend ourselves against the changing, decaying, growing, birthing, dying process of life itself. But "holding on" doesn't work in the long run. In our hearts, we all know this. Every spiritual tradition of which I'm aware, at one point, says: The Way is to let go, to surrender. In order to authentically let go, try practicing *letting be, first*, and see what happens. My experience is that after I've "let be" for a while, then I naturally come to an authentic letting go. But I have to let be, first.

And, it's also good to remember that "letting be" is necessary for accepting life's joy, too. In the multitasking, fast-paced reality of modern life, we often miss the little moments of happiness and gratitude. The practice of *letting be, first,* of fully taking in life's lessons—be it tea with your fears or laughter at life's cosmic jokes and irony—is a potent way to ground yourself in a more authentically realized life. And, it's generally the first step of legitimately "letting go" as well.

The Sacred Ground Beneath

Through cultivating the spiritual courage to experience our more painful and fearful emotions, we begin to touch upon the profound joy of life as life truly is. This is a recurring theme within any maturing spirituality: *Even when our life circumstances are fearful and uncomfortable, a joy of authenticity remains because we are no longer seeking spiritual awareness to amputate the pain from the picture, but to touch the sacred ground beneath all circumstances.*

It's there, that sacred ground.

And it is the tastiest fruit of any maturing, authentic spirituality, regardless of which religious tradition you follow to sow your seeds.

22

Innocent Misunderstandings

A famous Zen master once described his spiritual practice as "one mistake after another." The Christian adage, "we've all fallen short" implies the same. A Tibetan lama referred to his particular path as "one insult after another." How about you? How do you imagine your mistakes and misunderstandings along the way?

WINTER, 1989. IT WAS MY GREATEST FAILURE AS A CARE provider. Marcia, a twenty-two-year-old woman with leukemia, just a girl really, died only weeks before I was to start my internship as a hospital chaplain. It was Marcia's dying that first stripped me of my arrogant belief that "I knew" what healing was about, and to where I thought healing should ultimately lead us.

We'd begun our weekly support group in Dallas at the height of the pop-psychospiritual self-healing (read, positive-thinking) movement. It's easy to malign the pop positive-thinking movement of the late 1980s as overly simplistic (because often it was) and not too deeply grounded in psychological reality (because often it wasn't), but . . . still. At the time, this was the *only* belief system that offered many of us with a terminal or life-threatening diagnosis some hope of survival once modern medicine had given up. Nothing else seemed to offer hope.

Our support group emphasized the standard positive-thinking practices: speaking only in positive terms, declaring affirmations as to how "perfect, whole, and complete" we each already were, doing guided visualizations and meditations that focused exclusively on "love and light." Those of us core members of the group believed we'd found "the answer." Salvation was at hand, and the key was within our own positive thinking. And it seemed to work. At first. But such a simplistic way of looking at life's experience goes only so far before the shadows of a denied complexity arise. It wasn't long before several of our group members began to grow sicker and then began to enter the dying process itself. More than a few people came to me in shame and disgrace, thinking themselves to be positive-thinking failures as their diseases progressed. First a young man with AIDS died, and then Marcia relapsed. Marcia was in and out of the hospital for several weeks before coming home to die. And even though I was beginning to feel uneasy about the shaming side of our blind "love and light" philosophy, I hadn't yet begun to seriously re-evaluate my beliefs. My experience with Marcia's dying, however, would rip the Gospel of Positivism in half and force me into the then radical move of trying to embrace fear and the other "negative" emotions as legitimate, even powerfully potent, experiences within my own spiritual odyssey.

Marcia's mother called me early that winter morning. "Marcia's about to pass away. That's what the doctor says. So if you want to see her, you'd better come today." When I arrived, her mother warned me that Marcia couldn't speak, but she was still aware of her surroundings, still conscious.

Marcia didn't seem to notice when I first entered the dim room. But as I sat on the bed's edge, her eyes flicked my way.

"Hey, Marcia," I whispered. I was so scared, didn't know what to say. What positive thought could I possibly give her? What hope could I offer for recovery? It didn't occur to me that I might apologize to her for any pain or guilt I'd caused her by my either/or positive-thinking fundamentalism. It didn't occur to me that I might be honest about how scared I was at her dying, that I could witness to her my own fearful humanity. That's what I would do today: keep my belly soft, heart and face open, try to speak the truth, to really connect and let our souls touch. Today I'd try to be as honest I could with my old friend and ask for her forgiveness, tell her it's okay to leave us now, that I believe physical death is only one point along a larger journey. But, then, I wasn't yet able to be that truthful or courageous. I just sat there beside her, still trying my best to think positively (and failing), and to smile (so frozen and phony).

"Well." That was the second thing I said. Then I added, "It's okay."

"It's going to be okay," I repeated, smiling a plastered-on smile, nodding my head like I knew something big and secret that I was sharing with her. "Yes, okay," I said slowly.

Inside I knew I was lying. The last thing I would say to Marcia was a lie. Then I squeezed her hand, stood, and turned to leave.

Though she couldn't speak, she'd not been passive toward my presence. She'd stared right into my eyes. She'd stared at me with such a vehement, passionate hatred. Every breath I made seemed to disgust her. Every move, gesture, and word, a profound insult. She eagerly loathed me—*me* in particular, the "healing facilitator" who could keep a smile and an upbeat attitude in the midst of her almost unbearable agony.

And, if I'm honest, I, too, was furious at that moment, furious at her. It was that stare she gave me, a stare of her own anger and sickening pity that so well reflected how utterly empty and superficial was my care. She threw my own fears back into my face, like a splash of acid, eating away my outer layer of faux enlightenment to reveal the trembling fear of my own dying that awaited just beneath the placid, calm false assurance. So at that moment I hated her back, because I hated that fearful part of myself she revealed to me. At the time, my spiritual belief system made no room for me to have compassion or tolerance toward these all-too-human emotions. Instead, "fear" had become idealized as the modern Satan.

Marcia's legacy was a lasting one for me. Her overt, unabashed hatred and rage haunted me more persistently than any ghost, whispering in icy, deliberate tones, "There must be another way than this, there must be."

Within a month I would begin my internship. This experience with Marcia, a miserable failure of care, was the deciding factor in my decision to carry through with my earlier commitment to this internship, and to begin looking at my own fear of dying with honesty and openness. There had to be another way to live with life's great fears. There just had to be. As I look back from my awareness now, I can see how this failure of care with Marcia signaled the conscious beginnings of my odyssey's deepening. It would be a turn in the journey that recognized a necessity of traveling into the underworld of human fear, where grace is not idealized as something apart from life's grit.

I see it now, but couldn't then. It's been a long road since . . . of self-forgiveness and honesty. Of willingness to cop to my misunderstandings and many mistakes along my own life's way.

It is tempting to believe that if *part* of our religious understanding can be mistaken, then *all* of it must be. This dynamic of all-or-nothing righteousness can be easily seen in most fundamentalist point of view, which insists that the entirety of scripture be literally correct in teaching—that every word be "right" for us today, regardless of the historical and cultural context from which the text arose. In any kind of fundamentalism, be it Christian, Hebrew, Muslim, or even New Age, there is rarely any room to be simply *mistaken*. Though it's easy for us to mock the naiveté of this kind of narrow as pointed out earlier, it is far more difficult to recognize the very same dynamic at work in our own more sophisticated, liberalized forms of spiritual seeking; but it's here nevertheless. Our own narrow "either/or" sense of righteousness can keep its hold upon us in the most subtle of ways, especially when we don't actively work to acknowledge how mistaken we've been in the past—and, so, make room for our being mistaken in the present, or future.

And here is the real pisser:

As we follow an authentic path of spiritual investigation, our inadequacies will seem to grow. Our past mistakes and previous misunderstandings—spiritual and otherwise—become even more glaring.

It's infuriating at first. At least it was for me. I expected that my dedication to spiritual seeking, to growth, would bring about a greater sense of peace. Instead, just the opposite was happening; I was being faced with the likes of Marcia's anger and my own overwhelming fears. Suddenly, I'd become aware of my shortcomings with an intensity like I'd never before experienced. The reality is that, as we awaken spiritually and psychologically, we usually don't like what we're waking up to. Committed to a path of self-honesty and openness, we are no longer seeking to hide from ourselves, but instead are developing the will to look deeper into the aspects of our experience we had heretofore kept hidden or ignored. Again, this part of the journey can be extremely painful and, here as much as ever, we need good guidance, authentic help, and comfort. We need to know we are not alone. That all sincere seekers go through this kind of critical self-awakening. Again and again . . .

This is why I've taken to heart the concept and phrase "innocent misunderstandings," which as far as I know was coined by American Buddhist nun Pema Chödrön. She believes our past mistakes and errors along the spiritual path are, without exception, misunderstandings and—this is essential—they've been *innocent*. We didn't really know better at the time. Had we truly known better, we'd have done better. Thinking of our previous mistakes and errors in judgment as *innocent misunderstandings* allows us the freedom to examine our path with compassion, openness, and honesty.

Sacred Individuality, Revisited

And have no doubt that, while traveling a path that honors and encourages your sacred individuality—your honest fearfulness as well as wonderfulness—you will indeed journey astray at times. Such an endeavor is *not* the safe way, *not* the road most traveled by. For, unlike a teaching that refuses to admit its missteps and wrong turns, a path of sacred individuality remains open and willing to learn. Such a path offers and includes a sense of permission that allows you to acknowledge your misunderstandings of the past, and so more quickly recognize any misunderstanding in the present. Such an open-minded path allows you to continue to grow, to continue to evolve in spiritual awareness. An ongoing journey.

Let me say it again, in another way, because I believe this is so very, very important: An authentic path whose faith is large enough to encompass life's grit and still believe—believe in God's love and grace, believe in the sacredness of human spirit and individuality—acknowledges and honors the reality of our *innocent misunderstandings*. Now, this isn't meant to absolve a seeker from taking personal responsibility for his or her actions. In my own past, it's had the opposite effect. Because I am better able to look more honestly at my mistakes, I'm better able to try to make an amends, if possible. To set things right if I can.

We need to remember that our misunderstandings in matters of soul or spirit do not signify that we're bad seekers. And it certainly doesn't mean our seeking has been in vain. To the contrary, it affirms we are upon an honest pilgrimage; we are human beings who are susceptible to the very same traps, perils, and pitfalls of every other seeker who travels a conscious path. A famous Zen master once described his spiritual practice as "one mistake after another." The Christian adage, "we've all fallen short" implies the same. A Tibetan lama once described his own path as "one insult after another." Honoring the truth of your innocent misunderstandings means you're honest and that you have cultivated the soft courage to admit your fearful human failings. Everyone has been mistaken about some aspects of their judgment, their actions, and deeds.

Here, Jesus' words to the crowd who was about to stone a prostitute resound their truth: "Who among you hasn't missed the mark? Who among you has not been wrong yourself? Let him who has never missed the mark step forward now and throw the first stone?" I think it is wise to remember that Jesus was a man who practiced what he preached, and to notice that neither did he step forward nor did he throw the first stone. Something outrageous to consider, don't you think?

AN HONEST SEEKER WILL ACKNOWLEDGE THAT, YES, WITHOUT a doubt, he or she has been mistaken before when it comes to spiritual matters. And this is also to acknowledge that, yes, I'll most likely will be mistaken again, from time to time. As you mature along your chosen path, try to cultivate this quality of self-honesty. This taste of truthful acknowledgment and confession will nourish your soul's individuality well.

If we view our spiritual maturation in this spacious, process-oriented light, we can learn from our *innocent misunderstandings* and, like the Zen master, see our mistakes as continuous opportunities to awaken. Ongoing opportunities, one after another.

23

Practicing Without Preaching

When we walk the walk of authentic honesty of heart, and sincerely practice our spirituality without the noise of our own preaching, we create the possibility to share an intimacy far beyond words.

A MEDITATION TEACHER TELLS THE STORY OF A YOUNG woman who, shortly after becoming a Buddhist, struggles with the continued disapproval from her fundamentalist Christian parents. Over time, however, the woman comes to learn an important lesson: "My parents hate me when I'm a Buddhist, but they love me when I'm a Buddha."

This is one of the great lessons of any spiritual tradition—Christian, Jewish, Hindu, Muslim, New Age, Native American, you name it. It is a universal truth about the spiritual pilgrimage. When we rely on rigid idealistic spiritual identity, we often miss the true essence of the teaching, and usually separate ourselves from others whose beliefs differ from our own. Whereas, when we walk the walk of authentic honesty of heart, and sincerely practice without the noise of our own preaching, we create the possibility to share an intimacy far beyond our words.

My parents hate me when I'm a Buddhist, but they love me when I'm a Buddha.

This teaching also reminds us of an experiential truth: Often we are so busy being self-identified with spiritual labels and preaching about our way to others, we forget to simply, authentically be. We forget to walk with honesty of heart and live the spirit of the teachings themselves. Of course, there are appropriate times to speak out, to teach, or preach about your way to others. Without a doubt. But a mature spirituality asks us also to seriously cultivate *practicing without preaching.*

And, in this spirit, I think I'll let the commentary go at that—no further preaching here about *practicing without preaching.* Instead, some questions to contemplate . . .

Can you practice the presence of Christ consciousness without preaching Christianity? Can you practice the presence of Buddha nature without preaching Buddhism? Can you practice the presence of your chosen spiritual tradition without being busy trying to sell your spiritual agenda to others?

Questions requiring no answer. Just asking. Just honest contemplation.

24

Resting in Mystery

Finally, it's just too big a journey to ever get beyond being astounded, being surprised by the mystery. And so as we mature spiritually we come to recognize that we really have no choice but to settle down and rest in the mystery. To kick off our running shoes, sit back, and rest awhile.

AS WE CONTINUE ANY EXPLORATION OF THE SACRED, IT is helpful to keep in mind just how uncontainable, full of paradox, mystery, and awe, this human life pilgrimage of ours truly is. And we recognize the need to move beyond "seeking" for answers, and into "resting" within the questions and unknowingness of that huge, mysterious adventure we call life. Again, we return full circle to the child's sense of awe and are reminded that a great cosmic mystery is always among us. Right here, right now.

While writing these stories and reflections, I have tried to honor this greater mystery of the sacred, or "cloud of unknowing" as early Christian monks, the Desert Fathers, called it. What I've come to believe is that our journey here is filled with obscurities and clouds of unknowing, and this is intentional. The way to God, or wholeness, or Christ, or Buddha nature, or whatever you call "the Sacred," can never be truthfully expressed in absolute or concrete formulas for spiritual success. The game is never that simple, nor clear. Paradoxes abound. Each moment of our lives contains a deeper mystery. To truthfully travel "within" is a journey that is somewhat different and unique for each soul. In the final analysis "the Sacred" remains a mystery too big for our conceptual minds and intellectual constructs—too big for the letter of the law, regardless of tradition. Throughout this book it has been my intention to further the mystery instead of falsely claiming to solve it.

As many seekers have matured in their own spiritual traditions, they have come to see how the different "answers" they once believed are, in truth, only "points" along the journey—not final resolutions or an "end" in themselves. Each one-time answer had to be given up or grown beyond or integrated or, at the very least, given a lot more space to breathe. I try to take as a reminder the advice of Rilke from his *Letters to a Young Poet*, ". . . have patience with everything unresolved in your heart and try to love *the questions themselves* as if they were locked rooms or books written in a very foreign language. Don't search for the answers, which could not be given to you now, because you would not be able to live them. And the point is to live everything. *Live* the questions now."

And so I ask for your forgiveness if, despite my declared

intent, I have managed to sneak an answer or two into this book through the back door. Because I can only guarantee you one thing. Any "answer" I have now will one day be slowly burned, and I will have to return to the great cloud of unknowing and mist of mystery, to living within the bigger question.

"I Crochet"

One of my all-time favorite stories about the quality of *resting in mystery* comes from the Harvard psychologist, Richard Alpert, Ph.D., who gave up his academic career in the mid-1960s in order to follow his spiritual bliss, trekking around India looking for a guru. Alpert eventually found his teacher and was, as is the Hindu tradition, given a spiritual name. He now goes by that name, Ram Dass. (Alpert/Ram Dass's journey into India is recounted beautifully in his now classic memoir, *Be Here Now*.) My favorite story, however, is not from the book itself, but from a time later, after its publication and after Ram Dass had returned to the United States.

The story is from Ram Dass's beginning days on the spiritual lecture circuit. Remember, this was still in the early 1970s, well before such alternative kinds of spirituality became part of mainstream popular culture as they have today. Then, as he says, those who attended his lectures were mostly an homogenous group. Most were under the age of twenty-five, dressed in white, wore sandals, considered themselves devotees of one or more Eastern gurus, ate vegetarian, and used psychedelic hallucinogens to achieve ecstatic experiences. At one of these lectures, just as Ram Dass was speaking about the mystical states induced by meditation, he noticed that an elderly lady was sitting in the front row of the auditorium, listening intently to his every word. She wore black oxford shoes, a floral print dress, a hat adorned with fake plastic cherries. As he spoke, he also noticed that her head was continually nodding in agreement to *everything* he was saying.

"She can't possibly understand what I'm talking about," he thought. "Just look at her." So as an experiment, he began to speak of his own experimentation with various psychedelic mushrooms, and the ecstatic spiritual revelations that followed. Still, the hat of plastic cherries nodded in understanding. No matter how outrageous his stories became, the hat with the plastic cherries nodded in agreement and understanding. "How could she know?" he thought. Certainly, by the standards of his day and audience, practically everything about this woman was spiritually incorrect—the shoes, the dress, her age, and, of course, that hat. No matter how wild his stories of spiritual seeking and mysticism became, the hat of plastic cherries nodded knowingly.

After the lecture, as a small crowd gathered around the podium to personally greet him, Ram Dass noticed this lady with the plastic cherries on her hat was also standing in the greeting line. When she ventured to shake his hand, he couldn't stand it any longer. "You *know*, don't you?" he said emphatically. "How do you *know*?"

The elfish woman leaned in closer, giving him a smile of conspiracy. She whispered carefully, "I crochet . . ."

Ram Dass laughs when he tells this story. "I think that's when I first began to realize that the game is much bigger than we can ever possibly understand. Much bigger."

25

You Don't Have to Protect God from Yourself

Our own experience of divinity is intimately connected to our all-too-human reality.

FINALLY, IF THIS BOOK WERE RESTRICTED TO ONLY ONE message, one thought to ponder, it would be this:

Give yourself a wide range, a grand permission to fully experience this human life, the fear as well as the wonder; like the Tibetan saint Milarepa, if the inner demons of fear enter your cave of consciousness, invite them to sit beside you and take tea. Be wary of the censoring mind that says, "Don't feel this, it's spiritually incorrect"; instead, go deeper into those feelings and see where the journey leads you. You have a unique soul that calls out for creative expression through your individual human life. Try to hear its call more clearly and feel its pull into the larger experience of a whole life; as Psalm 139 reminds us, God is not only in the heights of spirit's heaven, but the depths of your particular human bed. In short, you don't have to protect God from yourself.

God wants to know you, so why not let God know you? God wants to feel you, so why not let God feel you?

It's my deepest conviction, my most intimate personal realization: In order to invite God to sit with me and take tea beside the fire of awareness, I must also invite in my fears, frailties, and other inner psychic demons. Because to invite in God only partially—say, to invite in only my predetermined spiritually correct ideals—is to exclude God's wholeness; and, as the mystics of our varied spiritual traditions teach, God is a wholeness so big we can't possibly conceive of It. I believe this is what Jesus was modeling when He insisted that everyone, including spiritually incorrect outcasts of His day, from prostitutes and lepers to Caesar's crooked tax collectors, be invited under the big tent of intimacy that He called the "kingdom of God." Yes, to my mind, *that* radical path of permission is the model, or the real-life walk, that is the authentic challenge of Christianity's teaching.

Of course this emphasis upon a radically inclusive intimacy is certainly not limited to Christianity. The great Zen master Dogen, founder of Soto Zen Buddhism, put it in no lesser terms than, "To be enlightened is to be intimate with all things." We are here to cultivate and explore our intimacy with all things: with one's own self, with our brothers and sisters, with community, with the natural world, and with God. The reality is we are wonderfully, fearfully made, and our experiences dance between the two. A deepening spirituality consciously seeks an intimacy with *both* the wonderful and the fearful, both the lightness and darkness within ourselves. As far as I understand it, this is the inescapable work of spiritual maturation.

And, believe me, I know: This sounds good on paper. But to begin to allow such a radical sense of intimacy and permission to actually enter our daily lives is hard, confronting, often ego-insulting work. Then again, what else is life for but to live fully, live wonderfully, and, yes, fearfully? Isn't it our responsibility, as God's children, to live up to our whole heritage?

The final story in this book is about my friend Chris who came to visit me for the last time in September of 1995. If you recall, Chris had an incurable AIDS-related infection known as CMV. He'd decided to stop taking medicines and let himself die naturally, but with the chemicals out of his system he'd also begun to feel better, to regain some temporary strength. Instead of lying around and "waiting to die," Chris decided he should act. "You know, give something back," he said. So during the last few months of his life, Chris joined a volunteer program that delivered flowers to terminally ill, hospital-bound patients.

I wrote about Chris's confrontational form of caregiving—how he'd get right up in your face until you understood he *loved* you—earlier in the chapter titled "Outrageousness."

What follows is the continuing story from that same final visit . . .

Christopher J. Hancock sat on the front porch and chain-smoked. "Will I go blind, you think? I can't stand that. My CMV's growing, you know. I can feel it. I hate that I might go blind."

He took a hurried, nervous puff of his cigarette. "But you know what I hate even more. I hate that now, right now, I'm only just starting to see what this is all about . . .

"It's all about love, you know." Chris said "love" slowly, in an affected way. Lov-va. Over enunciating, almost smacking his tongue and lips as if he had a mouth full of peanut butter.

"Lov-va. That's what it's about, you know. And I hate that, now that I see this, I don't have time to really live with it for a while. Know what I mean? Lov-va. That's it. That's what it's all about.

"I mean, I thought it was about everything *but* love. About how much money you had. Know what I mean? How many fine clothes. About your car, your house. How much sex. Know what I mean?"

Chris coughed and shook his head.

"But it's about lov-va. It's about going into those hospital rooms and looking right into the eyes of someone and not leaving until they know you love them. Until they see that someone else is there and cares. Lov-ves them. Know what I mean?" Chris pulled a long, slow drag off his cigarette, then laughed.

"I never knew that before. Isn't that wild? Never even suspected it was about lov-va . . . Know what I mean?"

Chris stayed with me for eight days. The week before, he'd been to Las Vegas visiting his oldest living friend. The week after this visit, he was going to see his parents on the East Coast, his last trip before returning home to San Diego to die. He was saying his good-byes.

The morning I drove Chris to the airport I was ready for him to leave. "If he'd only stop saying, 'Know what I mean?' " I'd confessed to a friend. "His need for approval is driving me crazy." The newfound insights dying had brought into Chris's life—and I'd heard them over and over—had begun to sound hollow, as if he didn't quite believe them or wasn't sure. As if he were doubting his own experience, constantly asking us for reassurance. "Know what I mean?" he'd ask after every insight, questioning me and himself.

"Know what I mean?"

Chris died in a San Diego hospital almost four months after his visit. But I remember that final visit like it was last week. "Know what I mean?" he'd asked.

"Know what I mean?"

I can see now how I wanted his near-death spiritual insights to be iron-clad, impervious to any degree of doubt or fear. And I can see now how I began to close myself off from his pain, which was my own pain, too. I can see how I wanted to exclude the unsure and doubting, those fearful aspects of his experience. And of my own.

Once again I forgot that the experience of one's own divine power—of "lov-va" as Chris put it—is intimately connected to our all-too-human experience.

I can see now how these are inseparable. One larger experience.

In real life, the only way Chris could become big enough to authentically feel God's love in himself was to remain big enough to feel the fear and doubt of his humanity as well. He had to be true to himself, fear and all. Chris was so beautiful that visit, his growing and reaching. He took so many emotional chances with me, showed his inner reality so nakedly. What an honor that was to bestow upon each of his friends as his final gift.

And, of course . . . of course Chris was scared and frightened at times. How could he not be? How could any of us not be? There he was, seemingly alone and dying, saying his good-byes to all his friends. Of course he wanted to know that he wasn't truly alone. Of course he wanted to know that someone else understood. Because if someone else understood, then he might, just might, not be so alone or crazy. And his life, his all-too-human life filled with many regrets, unfulfilled dreams and wishes, just like any of us, might have some deeper meaning after all. We all want to touch that, experience a bigger meaning to our lives. Know what I mean?

Like everyone, my friend Chris wanted to know he was connected to something greater, to God, even in the midst of his dying, his fear, his sometimes loneliness and questioning, in the midst of his being so wonderfully, fearfully human, so true to his very real feelings of the moment. Of course.

In my own fearfulness I forgot that then. But, I'm allowed to forget. A practice of permission *allows* us this. And so I'm also allowed to remember as well.

And I do remember the larger story now. The larger beauty of Chris's, and of my own, true experience here. Of every person's unique, individual expression of life here. Wonderful at times. Fearful at times. All of it. I remember the larger story now.

Know what I mean?

We are all,

We are all the children of

a brilliant colored flower,

a flaming flower.

And there is no one,

There is no one,

Who regrets who we are.

—Huichol Song

✺ AFTERWORD

As the novelist and philosopher André Malraux once remarked, "The twenty-first century will be religious or it will not be at all." We might understand Malraux's sense of the religious as including a personal, intimate sacredness that can arise within each of us and become manifest in our everyday lives. This is the way of cultivating spiritual maturity, of being true to one's own inner spirit and soul. When we close the door to our own imagination, to the unique and particular ways of how our soul expresses itself, we close the door to God's indwelling universal spirit as well. In this way, the journey into the Sacred is also a declaration of our freedom to be fully ourselves, true to who we are.

Yet I believe we cannot be genuinely liberated if we collaborate to keep others bondage. To be true to your own spiritual maturity means that you must likewise witness and honor the sacred individuality and spiritual diversity in your fellow human beings. There is tremendous power in being a witness. As we mature in our own sense of sacred awareness we begin to realize how impossible it is to keep this wisdom to ourselves. And, again, as emphasized earlier, this doesn't simply mean we go around doing the spiritual talk of our life's way; it means we authentically walk it for ourselves. We consciously encourage others, offering them a grand permission to discover their own particular, innate sense of sacred individuality. We witness for our friends, family, parents, children, lovers, neighbors, even enemies, the difficulty of their own particular path through this life. And offer encouragement, support, and respect. What kind of a world would we make if everyone became more tolerant of another's spiritual way, of another's particular eccentricities and bliss?

Just imagine . . .

What kind of community could arise out of a conscious endeavor to cultivate a tolerance toward sacred individuality and spiritual expression? Yes, ours is not only the way of the explorer who *travels within*, but of the activist who *witnesses without*. And so the power of a witness is profound. The witness offers hope amidst suffering without seeking to escape life's reality. The witness offers faith in a larger process of ongoing creation. The witness is God's angel incarnate, within each of us, ready to stand forth, a light unto yourself for all to see.

Speak out for your fellow pilgrims on this journey. Speak out for his or her inalienable right of sacred individuality. We need each other in this endeavor. Our individuality, uniqueness, and diversity is not an accident.

And so, again, we return to the same general refrain from three quite different teachers.

Gautama Buddha: *Become a light unto yourself.*

Jesus of Nazareth: *Behold, the kingdom of God is within you!*

And an anonymous choir director dying of AIDS: *I just want you to know if I could do it all over again, I'd be more outrageous. You know, give 'em more hell. Be more myself and less what everybody said I'm supposed to be. More myself, more myself.*

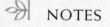 NOTES

INTRODUCTION

xvii *Jewish seeker Rodger Kamenetz:* this story is told in Rodger
Kamenetz, book *Stalking Elijah* (New York: HarperCollins, 1997), p. 3.

CHAPTER 2

12: *"He died of caner":* Natalie Goldberg, *Writing Down the
Bones* (Boston: Shambhala, 1986), p. 167.

CHAPTER 3

22: *"It is God's nature":* Raymond B. Blakney, trans., *Meister
Eckhart* (New York: Harper & Row, 1941), p. 243.

CHAPTER 4

30: *"Out beyond our ideas":* translated by Coleman Barks with
John Moyne, *The Essential Rumi* (New York: HarperCollins, 1995), p. 36.

180

CHAPTER 5

30: *"There seem to be"*: Chögyam Trungpa, *Crazy Wisdom* (Boston: Shambhala, 1991), p. 6.

41: *"Why do you"*: Rainer Maria Rilke, *Letters to a Young Poet,* translated by M. D. Herter Norton (New York: W. W. Norton, 1934) pp. 69–70.

41: *Robert Arpin in his memoir:* Robert L. Arpin, *Wonderfully, Fearfully Made* (San Francisco: HarperSanFrancisco, 1993), p. viii. Father Arpin, now deceased, was a Catholic priest living with AIDS when this memoir was first published. An autobiography composed of a collection of letters, it bravely and honestly confronts many of the issues facing the Christian Church as it begins to deal with homosexuality and AIDS, within not only its congregation, but also its clergy.

42: *Psalm 139:* Throughout this chapter I refer to the New International Version translation of Psalm 139.

44: *"Saint Francis of Assisi told . . ."*: Robert L. Arpin, *Wonderfully, Fearfully Made* (San Francisco: HarperSan-Francisco, 1993), p. ix.

CHAPTER 6

51: *"My son, Sam"*: Anne Lamott, *Bird by Bird: Some Instructions of Writing and Life* (New York: Anchor Press, 1995).

CHAPTER 8

65: *"softening the belly":* For a full discussion on this practice, including a guided meditation, see Stephen and Ondrea Levine's book on conscious relationships, *Embracing the Beloved* (New York: Doubleday, 1995), Chapter 22, "Softening the Armored Heart," pp. 112–117.

CHAPTER 9

77: *"There is a saying":* Chögyam Trungpa, *Cutting Through Spiritual Materialism* (Boston: Shambhala, 1973), p. 17.

CHAPTER 12

92: *Thomas Jefferson edited:* For more detailed discussion and to read Jefferson's abridged version of the gospels, see *The Jefferson Bible*, with foreword by F. Forrester Church (Boston: Beacon Press, 1989).

CHAPTER 16

115: *"And I'm happy that":* Martin Luther King, Jr., *A Testament of Hope: The Essential Writings and Speeches of Martin Luther King, Jr.* (New York: HarperCollins, 1986), p. 256.

CHAPTER 22

160: *"one mistake after another":* Soto Zen founder Dogen, quoted in Jack Kornfield, *A Path with Heart* (Bantam, 1993), p. 255.

CHAPTER 23

162: *"My parents hate me when I'm a Buddhist":* quoted in Jack Kornfield, *A Path with Heart* (Bantam, 1993), p. 309.

CHAPTER 24

165: *". . . have patience with":* Rainer Maria Rilke, translated by Stephen Mitchell, *Letters to a Young Poet* (New York: Random House, 1984), p. 34.

CHAPTER 25

177: *Huichol Song:* quoted in *The Fruitful Darkness*, Joan Halifax (New York: HarperCollins, 1993), p. 49.

AFTERWORD

178: *"The twenty-first century":* André Malraux, quoted in an interview with Michel de Salzmann, *Parabola 8*, no. 1 (January 1983). I'm indebted to Larry Dossey's book *Healing Words* from which I "lifted" this quote.

ABOUT THE AUTHOR

Joseph Sharp's writings have been widely translated, anthologized, and have appeared in various psychospiritually-oriented magazines and journals. His first book, *Living Our Dying,* was nominated for a Books for a Better Life award and translated into four languages. Joseph also served as an intern chaplain for terminally-diagnosed patients at Parkland Memorial Hospital in Dallas, Texas, and has been living with HIV for almost half of his life. His public speaking includes a diverse forum that exemplifies the sense of spiritual eclecticism and egalitarianism found in this book—ranging from talks at local churches, bookstores, and libraries, to lecturing at the University of Virginia Medical School and the National Cathedral. Joseph currently lives in Sante Fe, New Mexico, and is a masters candidate at Vermont College's MFA in Writing Program. He is also at work on his first novel. For more information on his upcoming lectures and writings, please visit josephsharp.com.